Bless me, Mother:

How Church Leaders Fail Women

Finbarr M. Corr, Ed.D.

Caritas
Communications

Corr, Finbarr M.
www.finbarrcorr.com

Bless Me, Mother:
How The Church Leaders Fail Wome
Second Edition

ISBN-13: 978-1539142911

ISBN-10: 1539142914

Caritas Communications
Glen Oaks Office Park
1025 West Glen Oaks Lane, Suite 106
Mequon, Wisconsin 53092
dgawlik70@gmail.com

DEDICATION

This book is dedicated to my wife Laurie Hutton-Corr, and her sister Mary Woodward, for their guidance and support.

Thanks to my fellow writers on Cape Cod, i.e., The Rising Tide Writers, for their insights and criticisms as I drafted this book during the past year.

EXPLANATION OF QR CODES AND HOW TO USE

QR codes provide real-time references in words, sound, and video - a three dimensional approach to publishing. By scanning a QR code (Quick Response), you will hear and see elements critical to Dr Finbarr's book. To scan a QR code, you will need a smartphone, iPhone or Android - phone or tablet.

No need to type URL addresses, just scan the QR code. You can obtain a QR reader at no cost on the either platform. Enjoy.

TABLE OF CONTENTS

THE COVER PAINTING OF FIVE WOMEN

Five women, who during early Christianity were put in positions of honor equal to men.

Priscilla (1st Century)

With her husband Aquila, Priscilla joined St Paul in his missionary journey and was instrumental in building the early Christian Church.

Phoebe (1st Century)

St. Paul refers to her as a "Presiding officer" and as a "deacon". She was responsible for the building the Church in the region of Cenchreae.

Monica of Hippo (4th Century)

Monica was mother of the great St. Augustine of Hippo. She was a devout Christian woman, married to a Roman official, an atheist, who refused to allow her to have their three children baptized in her faith.

Her prayers for her wayward son Augustine were rewarded, with his conversion to Christianity. His devotion to his mother is reported in the Confessions of St Augustine.

Catherine of Alexandria (3rd and 4th Century)

Catherine was a princess, born under the King Costus and Queen Sabinella of Alexandria. She received the finest education in the Arts, Science and Philosophy. She was committed to remaining a virgin, until she met a man who surpassed her. She found him in Jesus Christ.

Emperor Maxentius was attracted to her and when she refused to marry him, he had her imprisoned, whipped and eventually beheaded.

Saint Mary of Egypt (5th Century)

At a young age she ran away from home to Alexandria where she prostituted herself for seventeen years. She decided to go to Jerusalem and visit the Church of the Holy Sepulcher. In her memoir she records how some strange force kept her from entering. She was inspired by the Spirit to cross the Jordan and become a hermit in the desert.

INTRODUCTION

Many women were elated by former President Carter's latest book, *A Call to Action: Women, Religion, Violence, and Power*, published by Simon and Schuster in 2014. The Huffington Post commented, *"He demonstrates how he used his influence throughout his lifetime to push women's rights forward...Carter's book overwhelms—And as well inspires."*

Many women were enthused upon reading his book because, as several women said, "Carter 'gets' what "some" men don't. What "some" men don't get is seeing women as equal to men in the eyes of God. "He believes that his wife and other women deserve a faithful, loving and engaging partner."

"Theologically, he claims that women are to be treated with dignity in order to reach their full potential in all walks of life... including as priests. He feels that the Spirit moves within women...that we have voices to heal each other and our earth created by God."[1]

Carter's book suggests that the "plight of many women who are violated and suffer in the minefield where male domination, narcissism and violence of all kinds is rampant and, moreover, tolerated."

As this author has witnessed prejudice against women, so does Carter who concludes that discrimination, war, violence, distorted interpretations of religious texts, physical and mental abuse, poverty and disease fall disproportionately on women and girls.

Carter's urgent and informed wakeup call is supported by the late women's activist, a Dominican nun Sister Marjorie (Marge) Tuite, O.P., who taught her students and readers in the 1970's and 1980's saying, "Make connections between sexism and racism, between sexism and militarism, between sexism and nationalism, sexism and capitalism."[2]

Carter, as I do, supports the ordination of women and women's equality in all religions. Isn't it ironic that women are welcomed in many professions, but, in Carter's words, "are deprived of the right to serve Jesus Christ in the position of leadership," as they did in the early Christian churches? In the gospels written by men, the evangelists reported that Jesus broke the taboos of his time by treating women as equal to men. In Saint Paul's first letter to the Corinthians (11:11-12) he wrote "You need to learn that woman is not different from man and man is not different from woman and both come from God."

Whether you are a registered Republican, Democrat or Independent you have to admire Rosalyn and President Jimmy Carter. Which former president, Catholic or Protestant, would have had the courage to criticize the hierarchy of the Roman Catholic Church for excommunicating women priests, while pedophiles escaped similar punishment for two decades?

As a resigned Catholic priest and author, I am motivated by Jimmy Carter, a Baptist president, to endorse the movement to make women equal to men in the Catholic Church. I would love to see, during my lifetime, women ordained in the Catholic Church.

I will report on the Catholic hierarchy's abuse of the Leadership Conference of Women Religious (LCWR) and the Magdalene Women in my native Ireland. I will raise the question: If we had religious women as members in the United States hierarchy, during the past 20 years, would these women have chosen to protect the good name of the Church, or protect the innocent children, who have been sexually abused by priests? Like Jimmy Carter, I want to create a blueprint for women's equality worldwide.

PROLOGUE

Women and the Church

Growing up in Legaginney, County Cavan in the 1950s, with five brothers and three sisters, I didn't inherit the presumption, perpetuated in many cultures, that boys were superior to girls.

My mom, a college graduate, saw to it that, boy or girl, we each got equal respect. None of us boys, even the two of us who became priests, was allowed to lord it over our sisters. Unlike my mom, the hierarchy of the Catholic Church, which I love and served as a priest for twenty-eight years, does not treat men and women as equals.

In 1994, Pope Saint John Paul II, at the suggestion of Cardinal Ratzinger, his successor as pope, made it a matter of Divine Law and thus a doctrine that women cannot be ordained as deacons or priests. Later in this book we will review why the pope took this action, which was not a great surprise at the time. The bigger surprise to us progressive Catholics came when Pope Francis recently replied to a journalists question on the same issue with these words:

"With regards to the ordination of women, the Church has spoken and says no…that door is closed."

My sister Marie entered the Sisters of Saint Louis in Monaghan and eventually became one of the leaders of Religious Education in the Archdiocese of Los Angeles. Given my mother's treatment of all of her children as equals, I find it very rational to ask why Marie, a talented educator with a doctorate in education, wasn't considered equally as qualified to be a priest as her two brothers were.

Unfortunately, gender-based discrimination is not confined to the Catholic Church. It is evident from the testimony of courageous women from all parts of the world and from all major religions. As former President Jimmy Carter has written in his recent book *A Call to Action*, "There is a pervasive denial of equal rights to women, more than half of all human beings, and this discrimination results in tangible harm to all of us, male and female." The attitude of the Catholic Church towards women not only harms the individual but also harms the institution; leaves it deprived and doomed to fail in reaching what could be its full potential.

CHAPTER ONE

The Feminine Mystique

The reinvention of women's role in our American society began over fifty years ago, catalyzed by the provocative, perceptive and timely book *The Feminine Mystique*. The book was written by the founder of the National Organization for Women (NOW) Betty Friedan, who graduated *summa cum laude* from Smith College in 1942 and became a clinical psychologist. In the book Friedan reported that, prior to 1963, nearly half of the women in the United States, including her, were already committing the then-unpardonable sin of working outside the home. They were working to help pay the mortgage and grocery bills, but she admitted they all felt guilty about betraying their femininity, abandoning their children, and undermining their husbands' masculinity.

These liberated women were paid about half the wages that men received for the same jobs. They were passed over when it came to promotions, while their husbands routinely rose in the ranks and received raises. Friedan realized that the only ambition of many of her peers was to find a husband, marry him and have several children. In spite of her

1

training as a psychologist and a researcher in the social sciences, she married and had three children fairly soon after her graduation from college.

Quickly bored with writing about breastfeeding for magazines like *Ladies' Home Journal*, in 1957 she created a questionnaire and sent it to two hundred of her fellow classmates. To her surprise she found out that their education at Smith had not prepared them for the role they were trying to play, i.e., housewives, toilet trainers of their children, cooks for working husbands. She now had to admit that either their education was wrong or their role as adult women was wrong.

She submitted an article to *Redbook* about the survey's findings, including reports of her ongoing interviews of women psychologists, sociologists, marriage counselors. However, her male editors rejected her results, saying they couldn't be true. The editor of *Redbook* told her agent, "Betty has gone off her rocker. She has always done a good job for us, but this time only the most neurotic housewife could identify."

Friedan saw that she had only one option: to write a book. She knew it was going to be a tremendous threat to the whole philosophy of how women's magazines treated women. That book became *The Feminine Mystique*.[1]

Women had been trained for centuries to seek total fulfillment as wives and mothers and to glory in their femininity. Experts told them how to catch a man and keep him, how to breastfeed children and handle their toilet training, how to cope with sibling rivalry and adolescent rebellion. The female readers of women's magazines were subtly educated to pity the neurotic, unfeminine, unhappy women who wanted to be poets, physicists, or, God forbid, presidents.

Is it any wonder that many intelligent, educated women, like my mother, never had dreams of being medical doctors or college professors and were content to marry uneducated farmers like my dad? For some number of women, this life path was sufficiently fulfilling. My mother appeared to be totally happy in her vocation as wife and mother of nine children. In contrast, another of my female relatives finished medical school, never opened a practice, and became a very unhappy wife and mother. It is too bad that she was neither educated in the United States nor able to read *The Feminine Mystique.*

Friedan's book about the trapped American housewife became a national phenomenon. Serious family-oriented magazines and petty columnists were writing about it in the Sunday newspapers. *Look* magazine reported that 21,000,000 women were single, widowed or divorced and, even after age fifty, did not cease their desperate search for a man. Many married women told their therapists that they were bored or felt trapped in their homes with husbands and children.

Some of these traps were created by the women themselves. Freidan wrote that the "chains that bind the suburban housewife in her trap are chains in her own mind and spirit."[2] However, many of the research discoveries by Friedan and others about the American housewife were not published. Those few insights that were publicized were not used by therapists in their treatment of housewives because these new facts did not fit the current modes or thoughts about women.

As Friedan expanded her dialogue to include hundreds of women in the United States, many American housewives—as well as women in other parts of the world, found relief in speaking to her. Most of these women had thought their feelings of entrapment and wanting more out of life were unique to them. In this post-Freudian period some women saw their problem as needing more sex, but the reality was that there was something else buried within them as deeply as the desire for sex was hidden in Victorian Women, and today in celibate nuns and priests.

What Betty Friedan and her colleagues did was to create the New Woman in America—a woman who shared and also realized the dreams, possibilities, and ideals of yesterday's housewives. When the post-Feminine Mystique woman sent her children off to school, she felt free to pursue her own schooling and career, or to otherwise develop her talents without feeling any guilt about sacrificing her femininity or threatening her husband's masculinity. If any housewife didn't have the confidence to do this, she encouraged her daughters to pursue their education. My mother Nell, who raised nine children, three of whom were daughters, was influenced by the creation of the New Woman in the United States. She sent two of my sisters to boarding school (boarding schools in Ireland are the equivalent of high-schools in the United States) and my younger sister Dympna went to technical school.

The challenge for women to change was not easy. Friedan reported how difficult it was even for her. Even though she was one of the top students in her class at Smith and had won a graduate fellowship, she felt a strange uneasiness about deciding what to do with her life. She liked studying psychology and wanted to be a psychologist. She had difficulty forming an image of herself beyond college. She gradually grew from an unsure seventeen-year-old from a small Midwestern town to a confident young adult with the vast horizons of a whole new world before her. She grew to know the new woman inside her brain, knew what she wanted to do, and knew she could never go home to live like her mother and her mother's neighbors, "locked" in a home.

Friedan continued her interviews during the five years it took to write the book. In 1959, while interviewing seniors at Smith, she discovered that the question of career choice was still terrifying for girls. Most of the interviewees were seniors. Friedan noticed something different from her Smith class about this group of seniors: many more of the girls had rings on their left hand. When she asked the group what plans they had after college, those who were engaged spoke about weddings and work in secretarial jobs until their husbands finished school. The others remained silent or gave vague answers.

The next day one non-engaged student admitted that none of the students without rings knew what they were going to do and that "the ones who are going to get married are the lucky ones. They don't have to think about it." Friedan also noticed that some of the engaged girls became angry as the others talked about getting jobs, which she took as a sign of their upset that marriage would block their opportunities to make full use of their education. The "feminine mystique" was still very current in 1959; the public images and ads that sold washing machines, detergents and deodorants to women didn't help.[2]

Twenty years later, as women were struggling with the new equality they had won, they grappled with how to live it. They wondered if the developing backlash would prevent them from becoming the New Woman in the United States. How could young women on the eve of enjoying their newly won freedom reconcile their needs for love, children, family and a home shared with a husband? How could women, like my mother, who made home their career, face the future with self-respect and security? How would men, both single and married, liberate themselves from the rigid sex roles they had inherited?

The answer to all these questions cannot be resolved simply by focusing on the polarization between feminism and the family or between women and men. Friedan wrote about the need to take a fresh look at work itself, including the demands made by corporations, schools and government. In this book I will explore another essential dimension: our need to examine the way in which religions, particularly Catholicism, dealt—and are dealing—with the New Woman, both in the pew and in the convent.

CHAPTER TWO

The Promise of Change

T he Women's Rights movement in the United States began in 1848 with the Women's Rights Convention in Seneca Falls, New York. In 1890 the new National American Women Suffrage Association spearheaded the campaign to obtain voting rights for women. In 1903 the National Women's Trade Association was established to advocate for improved wages and working conditions for women. In 1920 the Women's Bureau of the Department of Labor was created to collect information about women in the workplace and to safeguard good working conditions for women.

At the beginning of the twentieth century women of the United States were searching for a new identity. Looking back at this period, women were forced to seek answers for their life's journey outside the home and the Church. The goal of the feminist revolution was not to become men, but to become truly human and be equal to men.

Helen Ring Robinson, the first female State Senator of Colorado and also one of the first women to serve as a state senator in the United States, wrote to the editor of the *Pictorial Review* in May 1919 that American women wanted four things: "They want a Fair Field in Sex. They want a Fair Field in Education. They want a Fair Field in Labor.

7

They want a Fair Field in the State." She added, "The greatest of these is a Fair Field in Sex."

Robinson claimed that American men took women less seriously than did the men in most European nations. She became more hostile, criticizing men and American journalists who disagreed with her writing. Referring to American men's constant brag about how generously they "treated" their women, she wrote: "Kind Sirs, you are suffering from a premature canonization."

Robinson was careful to keep her criticism balanced. She said that the leaders of American women shared the blame: the feminists rarely got down to fundamentals because they were reticent to get into conflict with men about "sex." Women seemed to think they had sufficient equality merely by achieving the right to vote on August 26, 1920. However, they still lacked economic independence. Robinson commented, "As long as women permit themselves to be pickled in sex, they will never be equal to men."

Senator Robinson encouraged women, especially feminists, to study sex as a force, a principle that strikes at the roots of being and rises in the act of living. Feminists, she wrote, "should indict how men dealt with the ferment of sex by mincing, deviling, dirtying and degrading it." Clearly, Robinson was angry that women allowed themselves to be dominated by men and kept subservient by society.

A key focus beginning in the 1920s was to establish a single sex morality for both men and women. Up to then, many selfish-minded men did not think of women as equals and took advantage of them sexually.

Robinson interviewed ten married men during one of her visits to Washington D.C. She asked whether women were entitled to economic independence. None of the interviewees could talk about women generically: they insisted on talking about "My Wife" as if their spouse was a possession. One gentleman responded, "I could not possibly love a wife who made herself economically independent of me." Robinson responded by asking the gentleman if he was confusing love with possession.[1]

The story reminds me of a recent discussion between two Vatican cardinals. Reportedly, one of them suggested that they probably should ordain some Catholic women as priests to level the playing field for women. The other cardinal supposedly replied, "Are you crazy? If you ordain women, then God forbid, one of them could be elected pope."

According to some psychological theorists, the history of men feeling and acting superior to women can be traced back to the story of the creation of Adam and Eve in the Garden of Eden. Carol Gilligan, author of *In a Different Voice: Psychological Theory and Women's Development*, wrote "if you make a woman out of a man, you are bound to get into trouble. In the life cycle, as in the Garden of Eden, the woman has been the deviant."[2]

Women's role in the Catholic Church in the early part of the 20th century were largely a subservient, domestic one. Growing up in our native Ireland, my three sisters were treated as equals with us six boys, especially by my mother in our home in Legaginney. That equality ceased when it came to how my sisters were treated at the local Catholic Church. Girls were not invited to be altar servers, and adult women did not serve inside the altar rails as lectors or distributors of Holy Communion. Women were not permitted to sit on the same side with their husbands in St. Michael's Chapel in Potahee. They were expected to sit in the pews on the left hand side of the aisle, Men were situated in the pews on the right and in the right hand section of chapel under the

9

choir loft. There was only one exception: Master Doherty chose to bring his wife with him, and they both sat on the right side. Nobody, including Father McEntee, seemed upset at the schoolmaster's decision, yet no one else broke the rule.

I remember how the laypeople in our parish of Ballintemple revered the male parish priest who was the pastor of our church. They put him on a pedestal. As a young boy, I remember overhearing a theological argument between two men, the older gentleman finished the argument by declaring, "I know I am right. Didn't Father McEntee say so from the altar a few Sundays ago?" To him and others in the parish, both male and female, Father McEntee was incapable of error in anything he preached, especially from the altar during the Sunday mass.

During that period of Church history in Ireland, most lay people completely deferred to their priests, a practice I believe that was adopted during the early Christian Church when the Emperor Constantine favored Christianity and thus helped it spread throughout the Empire. Christian leaders in turn assimilated some of the customs of the empire, especially expecting submission to male authority. In my own family my mother treated her brother-in-law, my uncle Father Lawrence Corr in a similar deferential manner and expected us, her children, to behave similarly. On days Father Lawrence was likely to visit, she would frequently instruct us to stay at home and not go fishing or go play football because Father Lawrence would expect to see us.

The historical development of the Church's relationship with women, which is reported in the New Testament, suggests that the early Church accorded women a more equal position. It speaks of the number of women in Jesus's inner circle, notably his mother Mary, who was held by the Catholic Church in a special place of devotion as the mother of our savior. Mary Magdalene is remembered especially as one of the holy women who discovered the empty tomb after Jesus had risen from the dead.

The New Testament reports that Jesus showed a positive attitude and respect for all women he met during his public ministry. In replies to the question as to why Jesus called only men to be apostles of the church he founded, theologians, Christian writers and historians don't give us many insights. One possible explanation is that, when Jesus lived on earth, Jewish women were subservient to men and didn't have the right to vote.

Apart from his relationships with his mother and Mary Magdalene, the best example of how Jesus treated women is recorded in the 8th chapter of the Gospel of John. The Jews and Pharisees confronted Jesus on whether the woman caught in the act of adultery should be stoned. Jesus shamed the crowd into dispersing them, one by one, with his famous instruction: "He that is without sin among of you, let him cast the first stone." This passage has been used repeatedly to demonstrate Jesus's respect for all women.

Another gospel story that reveals Jesus' respect for women's individuality and personhood happened at the home of Mary and Martha. The story tells of Mary sitting at the feet of Jesus as he preaches, while her sister Martha toils in the kitchen preparing a meal. Martha complains to Mary that she should instead be helping in the kitchen. Jesus intervenes and says, "Mary has chosen the right thing, and it will not be taken away from her."

According to the Acts of the Apostles, the early Church attracted significant numbers of women, some of whom held prominent positions in cultures that were not available to women in Judaism. According to author Alister McGrath, Christianity had the effect of undermining the traditional roles of both women and slaves in two ways:

- By asserting that all are "One in Christ" regardless of whether we are Jew or Gentile, male of female, master or slave, we are all equal.

- For the same reasons all could share the Christian fellowship and worship together. It didn't matter if you were a man or woman, Jew or Gentile, master or slave.

Suzanne Wemple (1985) reported that, even though Christianity didn't eliminate sexual discrimination in the late Roman Empire, it did free women to see themselves as independent personalities rather than as someone's wife, daughter or mother. Historian Geoffrey Blaney reported that women were more prominent in the Church in the Middle Ages than at any previous time in history.

During the Middle Ages, a number of Church reforms were initiated by women. A Belgian nun, Saint Juliano of Liege, proposed the feast of Corpus Christi to celebrate the body of Christ in the Eucharist. In the 13th Century, authors began to write of a mythical female pope, Pope Joan, while Saint Catherine of Sienna was an influential theologian in the 14th century who worked hard to bring the Avignon papacy back to Rome. The question now is why didn't this progression in women's roles in the Church continue in the following centuries?

CHAPTER THREE

The Challenge and Promise for Catholic Women

While the role of womens in the United States was experiencing a sociological transformation due to the influence of secular feminists like Betty Friedan and later Gloria Steinem, Catholic women struggled to live up to and accept the Church's stipulations and limitations directed at them, including moral teachings on sex and marriage.

Erika Bachiochi, editor of *Women, Sex and the Church* (Pauline, Books & Media Boston, MA 2010) wrote, "Classical teaching on abortion, sex, divorce and especially contraception are thought by many – both outside the Church and within—to reek of, at least, old fashioned ideas of sex, and, at the worst, patriarchal views of women. The reservation of the priesthood to men, for its part, is frequently regarded as male chauvinism. These Church teachings lead many to wonder how any self-respecting woman or woman-loving man can stay and pray within the Catholic Church."[1]

The Catholic hierarchy was taken aback by the widespread outcry after Pope Paul VI issued his encyclical on the Regulation of Birth, which was entitled *Humanae Vitae.* I vividly remember the day it became public, July 25, 1968, my birthday. I was in Ireland visiting my mother in a Dublin hospital, where she was recovering from an operation.

Mom noticed that I was not my jovial self and asked, "Finbarr, what's up? You are not in your usual happy mood today?" I couldn't lie to my mother.

I explained that I was very disappointed with Pope Paul's decision. The Pontifical Commission, which he had appointed to study the Church's teaching on marital love, had recommended that he leave the decision regarding regulation of the use of contraceptives to the consciences of married couples. Pope Paul ignored their report and proclaimed that each and every act of love between a husband and wife must be open to the procreation of children.

Mom replied, "Finbarr, you don't have to worry anymore. Since the Pope has spoken, it is final." I wished I had my mother's simple faith.

The dissent following Pope Paul's promulgation of the encyclical was widespread. Cardinal Leo Suenens was joined by theologians Karl Rahner, Hans Kung and some bishops in challenging the process by which the final decision was made. They claimed that the decision rightfully belonged to the College of Cardinals in keeping with the dictates of Vatican Council II.

Theologians Father Charles Curran and Father Bernard Haering led the dissent against *Humanae Vitae* in the United States. In spite of the protestations in the United States and Europe, the Vatican continued to condemn contraception as a violation of both the procreative and unitive meaning of the conjugal act. Even today, the majority of Catholics in the United States have a deep appreciation for the unitive meaning of the sexual act, but have little understanding or appreciation of the procreative significance of the sexual act in the religious context.

Bishops admit they are reluctant to preach on and defend *Humanae Vitae*. Bishop Kevin C. Rhoades, chairman of the United States bishops' Committee on Laity, Marriage, Family Life and Youth acknowledges that "the majority of Catholics do not know about the Church's teachings on married love nor understand why the Church considers artificial contraception immoral."[2]

An alternative to the use of artificial contraceptive devices is Natural Family Planning (NFP), a process accepted by Church authorities as totally moral for childbearing couples to regulate their pregnancies. Prior to the papacy of Paul VI, a scientific breakthrough in the understanding of the cycles of female fertility made it possible for committed Catholics to regulate their pregnancies by avoiding the marital act during the woman's fertile period.

Angela Franks, Ph.D, author of *The Gift of Female Fertility: Church Teaching on Contraception*, points out some of the positives and challenges of practicing NFP:

> *"It is important to understand that being able to redirect one's drive for intimacy into nonsexual expressions for a time is not a bad thing. Rather it fosters human flourishing—and thus is morally good. Periodic abstinence heals and integrates ones desires."* [3]

Others may interpret NFP as merely a tool created by a celibate hierarchy to control sexually active women.

In the age of Pope Francis it is difficult to write a chapter on the Church's promise to its women members, much less report on Catholic women's response to a Pope who apparently does not appreciate how hurt women feel at being passed over for ordination to the deaconate and the priesthood. According to Helen M. Alvare J.D., "Women never achieved in the worlds of work, politics, media, entertainment and business the sort of humanizing, person-centered influence that some secular feminists claimed they would achieve. But should the Church start down this path of integrating women into more fields of action, it will not only—according to its own theology—make God more visible in the world, but offer a revolutionary model for the world to follow."4

What does justice for the earth and creation called for in Pope Francis' powerful encyclical *Laudato Si* mean for the Church and its policies towards women? If Pope Francis continues to lead the Church as the Vicar of Christ for eight or ten more years and allows women's full integration into the hierarchy, he will likely find that no woman bishop, unlike male bishops currently, will choose to protect the good name of the Church over reporting a pedophile priest to civil authorities.

What if the pope envisions a Catholic world where men and women work together as equals? Husbands and wives would collaborate to meet each others needs, conjointly raise and educate their children, and share the cooking and caring for their homes. Part of the education would involve teaching children to live in a world where women are equal to men and not mere possessions of their husbands.

Family life educators like me are aware of the contribution the Church has made to feminism and have emphasized in our lectures that men and women are naturally oriented toward each other in a collaborative, mutually caring way. However, in spite of our teaching over the years, there is still a preponderant feeling among the faithful that men are superior to women.

This bias is more evident when you look at the monarchical, hierarchical structure of the Church. Reserving ordination solely for men may prove to be devastating to the survival of Catholicism worldwide. The question becomes, "Is the Catholic Church salvageable? Is its salvation tied in with the progress or lack of progress of Catholic feminism?"

Fortunately, we have a pope who recognizes the failure of members of the Church hierarchy to live up to their commitment to protect innocent children. Catholics were surprised that he appointed women to represent half of the Pontifical Commission for the protection of minors. In contrast to his predecessors, Francis is at least taking some positive steps by his appointment of women into specific roles within the Church. John L. Allen Jr., with the *National Catholic Reporter*, writing about the role of women in January 31, 2014, column, "Women are where the action is, as Pope Francis understands the action."

Those of us who love the Catholic Church and want to integrate women into its hierarchy should thank the Holy Spirit for sending us Francis as Christ's vicar on earth. He is the first sign that the Church is reaching out to integrate, and benefit from, the full range of talent, values and gifts of women in the service of our creator God the Father.

CHAPTER FOUR

Women In The Ministry of Jesus

Jewish culture in Israel before Christ was one of the most male-dominant cultures in the world. According to the Jewish faith, women had rights only in their home, and even there, they were limited. Men had ultimate authority over their wives and daughters: men governed women's activities and lives whom they could socialize. When a woman married, usually with an endowment, she went from the control of her father to the control of her husband.

Women were considered second class in the synagogue because they were deemed unclean during their menstrual periods. They weren't allowed to read from the Torah in the synagogue, and they weren't invited to attend any feasts or festivals. Jewish women could neither seek a divorce nor vote in elections.

When Jesus began his public ministry in 30 A.D., his teaching appeared very radical. He showed no partiality toward either sex. While Jewish women were not allowed to follow their rabbis, many of them, including prostitutes, followed Jesus. Jesus treated them with dignity and respect and elevated them in a world where they were often mistreated.

He gave no explicit teaching on the role of women in the Church. There is no record of his speaking of women as a class of people. He simply treated each woman he met as a person in her own right.

The Scriptures record his frequent attention to the plights of women. He forgave their sins (Luke 7:48). He healed Peter's mother-in-law (Mark 1:30-31), and he reached out to the grieving widow of Nain when he raised her son to life (Luke 7: 11-15).

When Jesus healed the woman whose body had been hopelessly bent over for 18 years, the leader of the synagogue chastised her for having Jesus heal her on the Sabbath, saying, "There are six days for work, so come and be healed on those days and not the Sabbath."

To which Jesus replied, "You hypocrites!…Shouldn't this woman, a daughter of Abraham whom Satan has kept bound for 18 years, be set free on the Sabbath from what bound her?" (Luke 13:15-16). By referring to the woman as a daughter of Abraham he acknowledged her equal standing with the men in Israel's religious heritage.

While Jewish customs largely relegated women to the home, Jesus pushed aside such discrimination on many occasions, such as when he talked to a woman at Jacob's well. The woman said to him, "I know that the Messiah will come, and when he comes, he will tell us everything."

Jesus answered; "I am he, I who am talking to you" (John 4:26). At that moment Jesus' disciples returned, and they were greatly surprised to find him talking to a woman. But none of them said to her, "What do you want?" or asked him, "Why are you talking to her?" (John 4:27).

Women were chosen for some of the most important roles in the life of Jesus. The first involvement by a woman was before Jesus was born. Elizabeth, wife of the priest Zechariah, was noted to be "upright in the sight of God" (Luke 1:6). She became the mother of John the Baptist, who later baptized Jesus and became his messenger. She was also the first person to learn that her cousin Mary was pregnant with a baby who would be Jesus.

During the sixth month of Elizabeth's pregnancy, the angel Gabriel was sent to Nazareth with a message to Mary. The angel said to her, "Peace be with you! The Lord is with you and has greatly blessed you! You will become pregnant and give birth to a son, and you will name him Jesus. He will be great and will be called the Son of the Most High God" (Luke 1:28, 30-32). Soon afterward Mary hurried to a town in the hill country of Judea and greeted Elizabeth. When Elizabeth heard Mary's greeting, the baby in Elizabeth's womb jumped with joy.

In the Annunciation story there is a strong emphasis on Mary's active acknowledgement and consent. This focus established a model for the validity of the role of women in decision-making.

When Jesus was grown, Mary was instrumental in his first public miracle at the wedding in Cana. When the host had run out of wine, Mary said to her son "They are out of wine."

"You must not tell me what do." Jesus replied. "My time has not yet come."

Mary then told the servants, "Do whatever he tells you." Thereupon, acting on his mother's suggestion, he changed six stone jars full of water into wine. "Jesus performed this first miracle in Cana of Galilee; there he revealed his glory, and his disciples believed in him" (John 2:1-11).

At the cross on Calvary, Jesus assigned Saint John to take care of his mother; and she was counted among his disciples after his resurrection, when they all gathered for prayer in the upper room in Jerusalem (Acts 1:14).

James A. Borland, author of *Women in the Life and Teachings of Jesus* writes, "The woman whom God chose to have the most extensive association with Jesus was his mother, Mary. Mary's life was significant for at least three reasons:

> * she was a first-hand witness of Jesus' divine origin and true humanity;

> * she was a tremendous model of goodliness, faith, dedication, and patience;

> * she, along with other women, was incorporated into the new life of the Church at Pentecost." (23)

In his analysis of Mary Christine Athans, B.V.M's *In Quest of the Jewish Mary*, reviewer Sidney Callahan notes that

> *"...according to Athans, Mary not only would have prayed, read and studied Torah with Jesus in the local gathering or synagogue, but in all likelihood would have been friends and co-workers with his female disciples. After the resurrection, Mary was present with the disciples at Pentecost and the birth of the church.*
>
> *Athans envisions the actual Mary as a strong woman of heroic faith working in the early church's 'disciples of equal.' In naming Mary 'prophet,' 'friend of God,' and 'truly our sister, who takes a leading role in church min-*

istry,' a Christian feminist message is delivered. A new understanding of Mary gives new impetus to the full and final equality of women in the church" (America, October 13, 2014).

When his parents took Jesus to the temple for his dedication as Jewish law required, an elderly prophetess named Anna was so excited to have lived to meet the Messiah

> *"She gave thanks to God and spoke about the child to all who were looking forward to the redemption of Jerusalem."* (Luke 2:38).

Jesus loved the sisters Mary and Martha. Once while Jesus was visiting them in Bethany, Mary sat and visited with Jesus as Martha was busy in the kitchen preparing a meal for all of them. Martha asked Jesus to have Mary come and help her. Jesus refused saying, "Martha, Martha! You are worried and troubled about many things, but just one is needed. Mary has chosen the right thing, and it will not be taken away from her" (Luke 10:38-42). His message to both of them was that spiritual growth and learning is more important than domestic duties.

Mary Magdalene is mentioned first in a list of the female disciples of Jesus Christ, which is extraordinary given that she was possessed by seven demons the first time Jesus met her. She followed Jesus from the beginning of his ministry in Galilee all the way to his death on Calvary. After Jesus' resurrection, she was the first to see the empty tomb. The first person he spoke to after he arose from the dead, she became the person to carry the good news to his disciples.

According to Sister Chris Schenk, "Early extra-canonical Christian writings show entire faith communities growing up around Mary of

Magdala's ministry, where she is portrayed as understanding Jesus' message better than did Peter and the male disciples... What is not disputed is the portrayal of Mary of Magdala as an important woman leader and witness in the earlier Christian Churches" (*Instituto Humanitas Unisinos*, Dec. 19, 2011).

It is not an accident that at a time when women couldn't vote or be legal witnesses, God and Jesus chose women to be the first and also the most important witnesses at critical moments in the life of Jesus (John 20:1-2). Elizabeth A. Johnson, CSJ, Distinguished Professor of Theology at Fordham University, notes that "in the early decades of the church there is strong evidence for a vigorous ministry of women spreading the gospel as colleagues with men...as missionaries, preachers, teachers, prophets, apostles, healers, speakers in tongues and leaders of house churches. They are co-workers with Paul and the other men, gifted with all of the charisms which were given for the building up of the Church. "Jesus restores women to 'full personal dignity before God' (Global Sisters Report, a project of *National Catholic Reporter*, *globalsisters.org*, May 1, 2014).

Author Edith Hamilton says the Bible is the only book in the world that looks at women as human beings who are no better or worse than men; however, the view did not hold. In the 13th century, theologian Thomas Aquinas, a Dominican, wrote "As regards the individual nature, woman is defective and misbegotten, for the active power of the male seed tends to the production of a perfect likeness in the masculine sex, while the production of a woman comes from a defect in the active power" (*Summa Theologica* Q92, Art 1). Unfortunately, Aquinas' negative attitude towards the opposite sex was also the attitude of the Church hierarchy by that time.

CHAPTER FIVE

From Feminism to Religious Life

While feminists criticized and rejected the historical and established form of religion, many envisioned feminism as a form of religion and developed a feminist spirituality, which was both personal and community oriented. In 1983 United States scholar Graham Gayle Graton wrote,

> *"If one believes as I do that feminism is a new world view, then the spiritual aspects of it has ramifications in every aspect of life."*[1]

The puzzling question for writers is to define female spirituality.

Katinka Hesselink, involved in spirituality, is frequently asked questions about female spirituality. She wrote,

> *"Most people talking about the differences between men and women have very outdated views about what women are capable of. I believe that most people are surprised that I am a licensed math and chemistry teacher."*[1]

Addressing the issue of female spirituality Hesselink writes,

> *I think the biological difference between men and women does not disqualify women from many professions. We are likely, for instance, to be smart enough to study math at as high a level as men. We are as likely as men to be able to meditate and inspire people...In my opinion the differences between men and women are relevant, but also far less important than other differences between people as a culture. We should take into account that biology and socialization are not as easy to distinguish as we think...I do think there are differences between men and women and how they apply to spiritual growth.* [2]

She goes on to report on how feminist anthropologists have noted that the greatest risk in spiritual growth for men is arrogance, whereas for women it is lack of self-confidence. In a latter chapter we will deal with the arrogance that is prevalent among the male hierarchy of the Church, who for years, maybe centuries, took advantage of religious women who lacked the self-confidence to stand up for themselves and challenge the dictates of the arrogant hierarchy.

From my experience as a therapist for priests and nuns, when the retreat master gave a homily for both nuns and priests warning them against pride, the nuns would take his words to heart and increase their lack of self-confidence, all the time thinking that they were working on their humility. Meanwhile the male clergy assumed the retreat master was addressing the nuns and that his message didn't apply to them.

I am amazed that our creator made us different but complimentary. In general, men can focus on a project and shut out all distractions.

I believe women by nature are more encompassing, taking all local situations into their circle of thinking, i.e., seeing the mess in the kitchen sink, a child needing a bath, and organizing an evening meal for her husband who is on his way home.

Some will argue that women have more social skills than men. It was obvious in our home. My mom would welcome the rich and poor, the highly educated and uneducated, and initiate a conversation. Dad was not as socially adept as mom. Mom expressed sympathy for the poor, the sick and those emotionally needy. She aligned herself with like-minded women, who would nurture each other, inspire and empower other women. By her life and devotion to individual and family prayer, she motivated my older sister, Marie, to leave a comfortable life, become a religious sister and make a difference as one of the most respected religious education teachers in the Archdiocese of Los Angeles, USA.

I would not describe my mom as a feminist, but I can testify that her spirituality and social skills motivated three of her six sons to go into the seminary, with the intention of becoming Catholic priests. My father thought I would become a hard-working farmer, like him. He thought I enjoyed farming because I would work hard in the meadow to finish a project by 5 or 6 o'clock, so that I could join my friends swimming or playing Gaelic football until it got dark about ten on a summer's evening. Dad didn't have the social skills to interpret my behavior like mom did.

I can still remember the shock in his face, when I told him at age fourteen, "I want to go to boarding school to become a priest."

Across the Atlantic, at this time a significant association of religious women was being created in the United States. The Congregation of the Affairs of Religious at the Vatican requested in April, 1956 that nuns in the United States form a national conference. In response to their request, a committee of nuns called a meeting of the major superiors of the various religious communities to meet in Chicago before the end of the year. They voted unanimously to form a Conference of Major Superiors of Women (CMSW) in order to "promote the spiritual welfare of the country's women religious." Their goals included increasing the effectiveness of their apostolate and fostering religious cooperation with all religions of the United States , the Catholic hierarchy, the clergy and Catholic associations throughout the United States. The statutes of CMSW were approved by the Vatican in 1962.[3]

The name of the Conference was changed in 1971 to The Leadership Conference of Women Religious (LCWR). The total membership was 1,500, encompassing 80% of the 57,000 women religious in the U.S., while 20% remained with the CMSW. The LCWR conference charter describes its mission as assisting its members to "Collaboratively carry out their service of leadership and to further the mission of the Gospel in today's world."[3]

The revised statues were approved by the Holy See in 1989. From then on two conferences of religious superiors have existed in the U.S. The LCWR contains a Vatican Council II reformed membership, while the CMSW contains a more conservative membership.

At the National Assembly meeting in Atlanta in 1971, a group of the traditional CMSW members split from the newly formed LCWR, accusing them of deviating from authentic Church teaching. The LCWR was not fazed by their behavior; they were captivated by the progressive spirit, enunciated by Pope John XXIII at the opening of Vatican Council II. (1962-65)

Since 1973, LCWR has carried out extensive programs related to transforming the perception of and about women. Sister Joan Kelleher Doyle, the LCWR president, reported at the annual conference in 1978 that "We have promoted the recognition that sexism is destructive for both men and women. If we choose to continue work on this goal we need to determine what options will most effectively insure images, structure and ways of relating, consonant with God's reign."[4]

The president of LCWR who showed the most courage was Sister Theresa Kane, RSM, president (1979-80). She was selected to address Pope John Paul II at the National Shrine, Washington D.C. on October 7, 1979. Her colleagues were shocked when, near the end of her address regarding the needs of her conference of women religious, she looked directly at the Holy Father and said,

> *"These intelligent, grace-filled women are not pleased with being treated as second class citizens. Why was ordination denied to these women while the male Church hierarchy focused on traditional Catholic issues, like abortion, premarital sex and being open to procreation versus using artificial contraception?"*[5]

Pope John Paul continued to stare at Sister Theresa, but chose not to respond to her. This was the moment in Church history where it became clear that members of LCWR had grown both emotionally and spiritually, as a result of their prayer life and assimilating the teachings of Vatican Council II, while their male counterparts, the Church hierarchy, were still stuck in a pre-Vatican II mindset of being anti-abortion and anti-sex.

From 1989 forward, the canonically approved LCWR began to influence change, studying the significant trends and issues within the Catholic Church and society. They used their corporate power to address any forms of violence or oppression. They identified with the oppressed and offered them resource materials to remedy their situations, while offering help to its members working as teachers in schools, and nurses and medics in hospitals. They made themselves available to the laity, offering help to those seeking spiritual guidance in their daily lives.

CHAPTER SIX

The CDF versus LCWR

T he Congregation for the Doctrine of the Faith (CDF) is the oldest among the nine congregations of the Roman Curia. It was formally known as the Supreme Sacred Congregation of the Roman and Universal Inquisition. It was informally called the Holy Office in many Catholic countries. Founded in 1542 by Pope Paul III, its sole objective was to "Spread sound Catholic doctrine and defend those points of Christian tradition which were in danger because of new and unacceptable teachings."

Because of the dedication of the missionary orders, the Catholic Church continued to spread throughout the world, and the CDF took on a more aggressive role, investigating grave 'crimes' perpetrated by both lay and religious against the Eucharist (Holy Communion), the sanctity of Marriage, the sacrament of Penance (Confession) and crimes against the Sixth Commandment (thou shall not commit adultery). These crimes came under the competency of the CDF.

While the Church hierarchy became more conservative, the LCWR assimilated all of the progressive directives from Vatican Council II and

exercised its leadership in a style one of its members described as…
"Transformational…a way of being in the world, but not of it." To
understand this attitude of leadership, LCWR regularly conducted
interviews with some of the more engaging, passionate thinkers–who
would give new insights into living a gospel-centered life. Some of these
outstanding thinkers were writers such as Walter Brueggemann, Judy
Cannato and Sister Joan Chittister. The spirit the LCWR appreciated
was that of Jesus, who overcame all obstacles and shattered the tendency
toward exclusion.

This is the same spirit Pope Francis describes when he speaks of
opening the doors to let Jesus out into the world.

Pope John Paul II lauded the membership of LCWR in 1986 saying,

> *"The Holy See (The Vatican) acknowledges with grati-*
> *tude the great contribution of women religious to the*
> *Church in the United States as seen particularly in the*
> *many Catholic schools, hospitals and institutions of sup-*
> *port for the poor who have been founded by and staffed*
> *by religious over the years."*[1]

"A distinctive aspect of ecclesial communion is allegiance of mind
and heart to the Magisterium of the Bishops, an allegiance which must
be lived honestly and clearly testified to before the People of God by all
consecrated persons, especially those involved in theological research,
teaching, publishing, catechesis and the use of the means of social communication."

This endorsement by Pope John Paul II had both a positive message
and a not too subtle warning, i.e., you are not an independent body; you
are subject to the College of Bishops, the Magisterium.

In contrast to the progressive spirit of the LCWR, who challenged the Vatican regarding the role of women in the Church, there existed a female religious Mother Tekla Famiglietti, who was a throw-back to the past, an orthodox leader who learned the political rules of the Vatican and used this knowledge to manipulate the all-male Roman Curia.

This 75-year-old head of an International Order of the Most Holy Savior of Saint Brigid (the Brigittines) since 1979 and a staunch traditionalist had built a strong relationship with Pope John Paul II and was among a small group of friends in vigil at his papal apartment the night he died. She cultivated global relationships with many different worldwide leaders, including Fidel Castro.

According to Jason Berry, columnist with the *National Catholic Reporter,* "Mother Tekla oversees a small empire of hotels, guesthouses, and restaurants from Israel to India and from Darien Connecticut to Assisi in Italy that brings revenue to her order…She is a unique and complex player in the global Catholic Church. She is often referred to as 'the most powerful woman in Rome' or 'popessa.'

> *"While being interviewed, 'she spoke in a demeanor that shifted from genial to steel-hard seriousness' and she seemed to sum up the entire journey of her life saying, We are a tool of history, but the one who really acts is God."[2]*

Another journalist described her as "a power machine, with high ranking connections in the Curia." By donating money to the cardinals to support their various charities, she was buying influence with the cardinals. Some of her behavior resembled the actions of Father Marcial Maciel Degollado, the founder of the Legionaries of Christ, who brought money in paper bags to Pope John Paul's assistant and gatekeeper Archbishop Dziwisz, in order to buy influence with his boss the Pope John Paul. The only difference was that Father Maciel was a very immoral priest, who had sexual affairs with several women which produced several out-of-wedlock children. His behavior was more than an embarrassment to the Legionaries, whereas Mother Tekla could only be accused, according to Jason Berry, of "Religious Capitalism."

Mother Tekla met Fidel Castro in 2000 during the inauguration of President Vincente Fox in Mexico City. She used her charm to get permission from Castro to open a small convent in Cuba, without discussing it with Cardinal Jaime Ortega in Cuba. A few years later she opened a larger Brigittines convent in Old Havana compliments of Castro. Cardinal Ortega boycotted the grand opening because he felt snubbed by the Vatican, believing they gave Mother Tekla permission to open the new convent without informing him or the bishops in Cuba. Monsignor Giorgio Lingua, an official of the Vatican's Foreign Affairs said, "Mother Tekla is not controllable." The Brigittines established four convents in Cuba.

The Doctrinal assessment of the LCWR, initiated by Pope Benedict XVI, continued during the same period. Seattle Archbishop J. Peter Sartain, an official appointed as overseer, attended their annual meetings and screened the presenters they chose to speak at their conferences. Many lay Catholics, both male and female, were angry at the cardinal's and bishop's treatment of the religious women.

In 2012, the LCWR held its annual meeting in Saint Louis, with 850 delegates participating. Their president, Sister Pat Farrell, OSF, addressed them:

"What we want is to be finally, at some end stage of the process, to be recognized and understood as equals in the Church and that our formal religious life can be and is respected and affirmed. We want to get to a point where there is an environment, not just for ourselves, but for the entire Catholic Church...for the ability to openly and honestly search for truth together, to talk about issues that are very complicated." [3]

The reality was that while the Congregation for the Doctrine of Faith (CDF) accelerated the disciplinary action against the LCWR, many sisters and priests were reacting to the climate of fear created by the hierarchy, who themselves were never investigated for causing the third greatest crisis in the history of Catholicism...their covering up the immorality and crimes of pedophile priests, sexually abusing innocent young boys. This same hierarchy was called hypocrites by a small but vocal group of critics, who asked,

"How could the same hierarchy that brought shame upon the Vatican by recycling pedophile priests from one parish to another, from one diocese to another and in a few cases, from one country to another, rather than reporting them as criminals to civil authorities? How dare they take the high ground and punish the LCWR, whose members have put their lives on the line taking the justice agenda of Vatican Council II to the poorest areas of the world." [4]

CHAPTER SEVEN

Nuns In The News

From 2010 to 2013 a growing number of films about the lives of women religious drew viewer attention. The period was a time of renewed interest about how religious sisters live and work. While religious women were assimilating all the progressive teaching of Vatican Council II and reaching out to evangelize the secular world, the Church hierarchy (cardinals and bishops) were regressing to a pre-Vatican II mentality. More recently "The Nuns on the Bus movement sponsored by NETWORK, and LCWR's dialogue with the Vatican has brought religious women within a secular spotlight and has sparked people's curiosity," said Charity Sister Rejane Cytacki of Leavenworth, Kansas.

Before his death in 2012, Cardinal Carlo Maria Martini, S.J., summarized the state of the Church: "The Church is 200 years behind the times and in need of a radical transformation. The Church is tired, and Catholics lack confidence in it. Our culture has grown old, our churches are big and empty, the church bureaucracy rises up, our religious rites and the vestments we wear are pompous."[1]

Cardinal Martini was not only factual but also prophetic. He didn't need to cite causes for the catastrophic fall of Catholicism. Catholic newspapers, like the National Catholic Reporter, printed stories of bishops who had failed to reach out to the victims of priest pedophiles and of a hierarchy who, by design, continued to protect the good name of the Church by moving pedophile priests from parish to parish rather than reporting them to civil authorities.

Two documentaries about religious women had the biggest impact on the Catholic laity: Band of Sisters focused on the social and political activism of American nuns over fifty years, and Trailblazers in Habits motivated young women to follow the footsteps of religious women who, in the post-Vatican Council II era, were busy evangelizing, teaching, and caring for the poor in ghettos and the sick in hospitals.

Band of Sisters contrasted powerful images of pre-Vatican II convent life with nuns' post-Vatican II life of activism for social justice, with a deep contemplative underpinning. Sister Rose Pacatte said, "This 65-minute documentary is filled with wonderful footage, photos and interviews about 'extraordinary women doing extraordinary things.'"

Sister Donna Del Santo,SSJ, a member of the Congregation of Saint Joseph Sisters from Rochester, New York, observes that the nuns have come into the spotlight under less-than-ideal circumstances. She said,

"I believe all the challenges generated by the Church hierarchy, like the Vatican investigation of U.S. communities of Women Religious and the LCWR investigation, to name a few…has helped people to see the injustices done by not recognizing the contributions made by women religious in the past and present. Nuns on the Bus helps to highlight this." She concludes, "Yet there is strength in the clarity of vision and commitment, especially to those on the margins, which our societies/communities desire from the witness of these women."[2]

Sister Julie Vieira, I.H.M., of Monroe, Michigan is excited about the films' stories. She writes,

"The Internet and social media have provided unparalleled access to religious life across the globe and across the genres of religious life… Film is a great way to dive more deeply into these stories as well as to explore spirituality, commitment, mission, community and other topics that are meaningful to people."

The question we must ask now is what did these documentaries and films on religious women achieve for the equality of women in the Roman Catholic Church? To date, the honest answer is zero. Meanwhile some of the same United States bishops who tried to discipline the nuns have completely evaded any disciplinary action for their cover-ups of wayward priests in their jurisdictions.

Jason Berry, a journalist writing for the National Catholic Reporter in January 2013, said,

"As the Congregation for the Doctrine of the faith accelerates a disciplinary action against the main leadership group of American nuns, many sisters and priests are reacting to a climate of fear fostered by the bishops and cardinals who (at this time) have never been investigated for their role in the greatest moral crisis of modern Catholicism: the clergy sex abuse crisis."

"A small but resonant chorus of critics is raising an issue of hypocrisy that has grown too blatant to ignore. The same hierarchy that brought shame on the Vatican for recycling clergy child molesters has assumed a moral high ground in punishing the LCWR, a group whose members have put their lives on the line in taking the social justice agenda of the Second Vatican Council to some of the poorest areas of the world."

"Many nuns from foreign countries wonder if the investigation of LCWR is an exercise 'in displaced anger,' as one Sister put it, over the hierarchy's failure in child abuse scandals across the map of the global church."3

The LCWR accusers have spotty records. Cardinal Bernard Law of Boston is a good example. According to the Catholic press and sources at the Vatican, he was a prime mover behind the "apostolic visitation" of the American nun communities. Several priests in the Archdiocese of Boston rebelled and demanded that Cardinal Law be removed. He resigned as archbishop in December 2002 and spent 18 months living in a convent of nuns in Maryland between his frequent trips to Rome. To the surprise of many lay Catholics, and also to the disgust of those organizations who were focused on protecting the victims of pedophile priests, the Vatican rewarded him with the position of prefect of Santa Maria Maggiore, a historic basilica. Meanwhile he left the Archdiocese of Boston in a "staggering mess." 4

One of the challenges that our Catholic Church has difficulty addressing is the condition of clericalism, which has affected Catholicism for centuries. Clericalism teaches male seminarians that they are aspiring to a higher level of existence unavailable to the laity. They are taught that their special sacred powers will accompany them into eternity. For such privileges, they promise to become mere jellyfish for the kingdom and promise to defer their own judgment without reservation to authoritative pronouncements of those on a higher level, be it pastor, bishop or pope. On the feast of the Solemnity of Mary in 2013, Cardinal Mauro Piacenza, head of the Vatican's Congregation for the Clergy, released a letter to mothers of priests and seminarians. He not only compliments the women in their role as teachers and examples of faith in the home but also states that "the entire church looks with admiration and deep gratitude upon all mothers of priests and of those who, having received this lofty vocation, have embarked upon the path of formation." Commenting on the letter, the National Catholic Reporter observed that Cardinal Piacenza wove "a top-heavy construct of unnecessary speculative theology about the priesthood, overlaid with treacly pieties and strange contortions of gender and familial relations." [5]

In contrast to Piacenza's encouragement of clericalism, Abbot Peter von Sury of Switzerland urges changes in the Church structures. Von Sury advocates that the changes start by returning to the voices of the faithful, the local clergy and the neighboring bishops in the selection of bishops. Von Sury argues that the Church is suffering from a "closed system" in which men chosen to be bishops will not challenge the status quo. A closed system is not capable of accepting criticism or correction from the outside. Von Sury's view is that the path towards ordination is filled with those who embody the outdated culture, which only produces more priests who see themselves on a pedestal above the laity. The last thing we need in the Catholic Church today is an enhancement of the clerical privilege. We need for our Holy Father Pope Francis and the male hierarchy to install women as deacons as a first step to abandoning clericalism in the Church forever.

CHAPTER EIGHT

The Role of Women In The Catholic Church

Many women play active roles similar to men in the Catholic church. They serve as lectors, Eucharistic ministers and ushers during Sunday masses but very few of them have sanctioned titles. Even the young women who answer the divine call and become nuns don't receive the blessing of ordination—only men can be ordained. The Eastern Orthodox Catholics, who ordain married men, don't ordain women.

When a reporter asked the popular Pope Francis, on his return flight from Brazil, "What is the possibility of ordaining women as priests?" the pope replied, "The Church has spoken and says NO…that door is closed."

That response was the pope's way of referring to Pope John Paul II's 1994 document, *Ordinatio Sacerdotalis*, in which John Paul said that the Church has no authority to ordain women and that this view must be held by all the faithful as a definitive belief.[1] The Congregation for the

Doctrine of the Faith headed by then-Cardinal Joseph Ratzinger soon issued a supposedly clarifying statement that, while Ordinatio Sacerdotalis was not an infallible statement, the ban on women priests is infallible because it represents the consistent and clear tradition of the Church. In the opinion of several theologians and this author, while the pope's document is definitive and demands acceptance by the faithful, it is not an infallible teaching, nor is any statement of the Congregation infallible. Most importantly Pope Francis does not say, "I fully concur with my predecessor John Paul's reasoning." The door may be closed but not locked; the light of the Spirit may be visible through the cracks!

I recently had an opportunity to communicate regarding the role of women in the Catholic church with a retired professor of theology. I will simply call her "Eileen" to protect her anonymity. I asked what her feelings were about the Church's refusal to ordain women, even to the diaconate. She replied by email:

> *"I fondly remember standing on the Grecian shore near Corinth where Phoebe, the ONLY deacon mentioned in the bible, supposedly departed for Rome bearing Paul's letter. Women were VERY active participants in spreading the early mission and vision of Christianity! The diaconate allows participation in church governance including the possibility of direct elevation to the status of Cardinal, as well as the authority to preach and confer most of the sacraments as part of one's pastoral ministry. I will never be able to forget my experiences during my work at a school of theology. In two separate courses, with two different (female) professors, the issue of women's ordination spontaneously arose within the context of our class discussion.*

On both occasions the professor rushed to tightly shut the classroom door, then reminded the entire class that under Canon Law no professor—or student—was allowed to even mention the topic within an 'ecclesiastically licensed' school of theology and could be automatically fired if such conversation occurred."

I wonder if Pope Francis is aware of these restrictions authorized by the Congregations who are under his jurisdiction. I also wonder if he is aware of the thousands of Catholic women like Eileen who passionately want the role of women in the Church to include the option of ordination to the diaconate, which would include sharing in the authority of the Church administration at the local level.

The historical facts suggest that Pope Francis approves an expanded role for women. A few months after his election as our pontiff, Pope Francis in an interview with Antonio Spadaro, the Jesuit editor of *La Civilta Cattolica*, called for a widespread and invasive female presence in the Church. The interview was translated into several languages and printed in 16 Jesuit journals. It caught the attention of the major Spanish newspaper, *El Pais,* which suggested that Francis might be considering female cardinals. Francis repeated the same call a few months later in his first apostolic exhortation *Evangelii Gaudium* (The Joy of the Gospel): "We need to create still broader opportunities for a more incisive presence of women in the Church."

The Catholic hierarchy seems to teach that they cannot reverse Jesus' decision to choose male, rather than men and women apostles to continue his mission on earth. The hierarchy claims to be following the tradition of the Church by reserving the ordination to the priesthood for men only. They teach and preach this discipline in spite of the fact that there is no evidence in scripture that Jesus "chose" and "ordained" priests. He chose and "commissioned" apostles; their successors were called bishops. The ordination of priests was part of the tradition created in the early Church.

There is another "new" historical fact reported in Saint Paul's letter to the Romans Chapter (16:1): "I recommend to you our sister Phoebe, 'diakonos' at the church at Cenchreae." ("I commend to you Phoebe our sister, who is [also] a minister of the church at Cenchreae," source: usccb.org) The word "diakonos" is generally masked in the English translation as "servant." This is the same Phoebe that "Eileen" referred to in her email to me. There is also historical evidence from secular literature that supports the existence of women deacons (diackonii) during the reign of Trajan (28-117 C.E.): "In Bithynia under Trajan there were female deacons;" and written on a stone slab, in the same period, is "*Sophia~he~diakonos, he~deutre Phoebe*"[2]

I am personally hopeful that Pope Francis will remember that there was a tradition of women deacons in the early church and that he will make a unilateral decision to restore this role for Catholic women, who are both spiritually motivated and emotionally ready to share the ministry of ordained male priests in their local community. Francis has already demonstrated that he is a staunch women's advocate. He has taken a stand for equal pay, calling the wage gender gap "pure scandal." He has emphasized reconciliation and forgiveness for women who have had abortions and who wish to follow Church teachings in good faith.

Recently, he streamlined the cumbersome and costly process of annulments, lauded by many as an act of mercy.

I look forward to a time when Catholic women will no longer be relegated to serving at the altar during liturgical services or serving on parish councils, which some women interpret as a first step to sharing authority with Catholic men.

We need to see women standing on the altar with deacon stoles around their necks, witnessing weddings and performing baptisms at their local parishes.

C H A P T E R   N I N E

Religious Women Shaping Theology

O ne of the religious women who played a significant role in shaping Catholic theology in the United States. over the past 50 years was born in Chicago, the oldest of 11 children. Sister Mary Ann Hinsdale writes in her biography [1] that she was influenced in her teenage years by movements like the Young Christian Students (YCS), the Sodality of Our Lady, and The Grail, a women's spiritual organization focused on peace, justice and renewal of the earth,

Mary Ann Hinsdale, IHM

During the time of the Second Vatican Council (1962-65) she was attending Catholic high school; and, as the Council ended, she entered the Congregation of the Immaculate Heart of Mary (IHM). Her short list of people who most inspired her includes the influential American psychologist Carl Rogers, the educator and advocate of liberation theology Paulo Freire, and social activist Dorothy Day of the Catholic Worker Movement. (Her only regret was never meeting Dorothy Day.) When Hinsdale read Sister Carmel McEnroy's book *Guests in Their Own House: The Women of Vatican II*, she was surprised to learn that women participated as auditors in the second half of Vatican Council II and had an influence in the development of the Theology of the Council.

Hinsdale's IHM congregation was a component of the Conference of Major Superiors of Women (CMSW). CMSW's general superior Sister Margaret Brennan professed that "if women were to have any influence in shaping the future of the Church, they had to be able to speak with an educated theological voice." This mantra motivated Hinsdale to pursue a master's degree and later a doctorate in theology. After achieving her master's, she taught Religion and English at a Catholic high school in Detroit.

She admits she felt slighted after Vatican Council II because the priests at the high school and parish had the privilege of concelebrating mass, while she was not invited to concelebrate. She became aware of a "false consciousness" and "ecclesiastical exclusion" because of this experience. Even though she had a degree in religious education, which several of the priests didn't have, she felt that the church hierarchy put male priests on a higher level than female religious.

During 1980-81 she spent two semesters studying theology at the University of Tubingen, one of Germany's oldest and most famous universities. While there she met the renowned theologian Hans Küng. Later, while studying at the University of Nijmegen found in the Netherlands she met other scholars, both men and women, who were enthusiastic about feminist theology.

Hinsdale received her Ph.D. in theology in 1984 and was drawn to the field of Catholic feminism. While studying in Europe she felt that she was right in the middle of developing theology, since most of the theological experts came from Europe (the only exceptions being Gregory Baum, a peritus at Vatican Council II, and Bernard Lonergan, both Canadians). Back in the United States, Catholic seminaries, once hostile to female students and female theologians, suddenly provided wonderful, if challenging, environments for female students and female theologians.

In contrast to her experience in Detroit, Hinsdale had a positive experience in 1987 when she served on the staff of the College of Holy Cross in Worcester, MA. The vast majority of the staff was committed to an inclusive, participative, ecclesial and ministerial vision, which was inferred by Vatican Council II. Many of her colleagues in the Religious Studies Department at Holy Cross were feminists, and nearly all her male colleagues, especially the chair Bernard Cooke, were well disposed to feminist and liberation theology.

Hinsdale summarizes her experience as a teacher and theologian in academia for more than twenty years: "First, I find that much of what shapes my own theology comes from the reactions and questions raised by my students; and secondly, I have begun to see that, what seem like setbacks in women's struggle to gain voice and agency in theology and the Church, often can become a source of grace and impetus for transformation."[2]

Rosemary Radford Ruether

Another female theologian, Rosemary Radford Ruether, obtained her Doctorate in Theology in 1964 at Claremont Graduate University while raising three small children. She says that reading the independent National Catholic Reporter newspaper motivated her interest in the renewal of Catholicism. Now a renowned feminist Catholic scholar, she has had a tremendous impact on shaping theology in the U.S. In her writings she recalls being motivated by Vatican Council II and the struggles for reform that developed out of it. She accepted a personal challenge in 1966 when she took the position of professor at the School of Religion of the historically black and male-oriented Howard University in Washington, D.C. Ruether balanced her teaching during the next ten years with writing books and social activism. In 1976 she joined the faculty of Garrett-Evangelical Theological seminary in Evanston, Ill. and taught there for 28 years. Two of her 36 books need to be highlighted here: *Religion and Sexism: Images of Women in the Jewish and Christian Traditions and Sexism and God-Talk: Toward a Feminist Theology.*

Sister Joan D. Chittister, OSB

Sister Joan D. Chittister, a Benedictine nun and best-selling author, as well as an outspoken advocate for justice, peace and equality, is a well-known international lecturer on several issues shaping the theology of Roman Catholicism. In her current role as the co-chair of the Global Peace Institution for Women, a partner organization of the United Nations, she facilitates a worldwide network of peace builders, especially in the Middle East. On a local level in the United States she is the founder and executive director of Benet Vision, a resource for contemporary spirituality in Erie, Pennsylvania.[3]

On November 6, 2015, Chittister wrote that Pope Francis should create a new approach to priesthood since many Catholic communities in the world don't see a priest more than once a year. She suggested that creating a married clergy as a complement to a celibate priesthood would be a vital and viable solution to priestless parishes. Her argument was that such a move would lead to an increase in candidates for the priesthood and would also make the Church's ministry to couples and families much more credible.

She added, "I am convinced that until the issue of ordaining women as priests (or deacons) is addressed by the Church, the number of active parishioners will decline and the Church will fail in the 21st century. If Christianity is ever to be Christianity again, we must admit that women are also full human beings and disciples of Jesus Christ."

Chittister wonders whether Pope Francis and the Church hierarchy have figured out the relationship between married male priests and the projected ordination of women priests. Commenting on events in my native Ireland she writes:

> *"A recent report on the public position of a group of Irish priests concerning the ordination of women puts the issue of women in the Church in a clear and penetrative perspective. They say, 'We are aware there are many women who are deeply hurt and saddened by this teaching. We also believe that the example given by the Church in discriminating against women encourages abuse and violence against women in many cultures and societies.'"*

What relationship, if any, is there between these seemingly different issues? What can the ordination of married men have to do with the ordination of women? Sister Joan concludes, "This new topic of a married priesthood, which is now in the Pope's diary, I think, if hearsay is correct, changes all that but not in the way most people might think. And that is my problem."

Elizabeth A. Johnson, CSJ

Elizabeth A. Johnson, a member of the Sisters of Saint
Joseph and a Roman Catholic feminist theologian, has made her voice
heard and her writing effective in shaping the theology of the Church.
Johnson is a distinguished professor of theology at Fordham University,
a Jesuit institution in New York City. Johnson is a high-profile theolo-
gian who holds numerous awards and honorary doctorates from
Catholic institutions. She has served as president of both the
Theological Society of America and the American Theological Society.

Her 2007 book *Quest for a Living God: Mapping Frontiers in the
Theology of God* won the first place award from the Catholic Press
Association in the "academic theology" category. According to the
Committee on Doctrine of the United States Conference of Catholic
Bishops, her book contains a series of "misrepresentations, ambiguities
and errors and does not accord with authentic Catholic teaching on
essential points." In simpler language, the bishops judged that
Johnson's treatment of the Trinity in Quest for a Living God "complete-
ly undermines the Gospel and faith of those who believe in the Gospel."
Even though the criticism was harsh, the Congregation didn't silence
her, forbid her to teach theology or impose any disciplinary measures.

In August 2008 Johnson addressed the Leadership Conference of
Women Religious (LCWR) and the Conference of Major Superiors of
Men's institutes (CMSM), the umbrella groups of women's and men's
religious orders that meet every five years. John L. Allen, Jr. reported
that Johnson asked her audience of fellow religious to "suck the venom"
out "of those wounds" so that "we can go forward making a powerful
contribution without hatred." Johnson reflected on the role of the Holy
Spirit building community within the Church. Quoting the Belgian the-

ologian Edward Schillebeeckx, she said "Catholics lovingly regard the Church as the only real reliquary of Jesus in the world."

She reflected on how love at times is tested by the Church's human failures. She criticized the hierarchy directly, saying "In our day the entrenched clerical system of patriarchal power, in addition to creating conditions in which sex abuse scandal could occur, has also at times been deeply suspicious of the charism of religious life and where it will lead the Church. I think of the Jesuits and Justice, of the option of so many women religious orders for a collegial style of leadership and obedience."

Hitting the hierarchy between the eyes, she continued "We in the Catholic Church continue to live by patriarchal values that, by any objective measure, relegate women to a second class status, governed by male-dominated structures, laws and rituals." Finishing her presentation on a positive note, Johnson added, "Jesus didn't come to die but live and to help others in the joy of Divine love."

Elizabeth Schüssler Fiorenza

Elizabeth Schüssler Fiorenza, a feminist and the final theologian discussed in this chapter, also played a leading role in helping shape the theology of our Church. Fiorenza was born in the kingdom of Romania in April, 1938. As the Russian army advanced through Romania, her parents fled with her to south Germany. They later settled in Frankfurt where she attended school. She received her licentiate of theology in 1961 and subsequently a doctorate in theology from the University of Münster. She married Francis Schüssler Fiorenza, an American theologian.

In 1984, Elizabeth was one of 97 theologians who signed a Catholic statement on pluralism and abortion, calling for religious pluralism and discussion within the Church of the Church's position on abortion.

Formerly at Notre Dame, she is currently a professor of Divinity at Harvard Divinity School. Elizabeth co-founded the *Journal of Feminist Studies in Religion* and was elected the first president of the Society of Biblical Literature.

In one of her earliest and best-known books, *In Memory of Her: A Feminist Theological Reconstruction of Christian Origins*, she argues for the retrieval of the overlooked contributions of women in the early Christian church. She also sets a high standard for historical rigor in feminist theology. To hone in on the source of gender equality, she turns to one of Saint Paul's core theological verses: "There is no longer... slave or free, there is no longer male or female, for all of you are one in Christ" (Galatians 3:28).

She reports that in Saint Paul's Christian communities women didn't have to become men to become holier, they simply had to follow Christ. From Elizabeth's perspective, what Saint Paul declared in Galatians confirms the legitimacy of women in ministry. [4]

CHAPTER TEN

What Is Happening In The Church Today?

T he last time I asked myself the question above was 53 years ago, when the elderly pontiff John XXIII initiated Vatican Council II and summoned hundreds of cardinals and bishops from all over the world to Vatican City with the invitation "Let's open up the windows of the Church and let in some fresh air." As a recently ordained priest, known as a progressive, I was very excited that the language of the Mass would change from Latin to the vernacular (English) and that the definition of the Church would change from an emphasis on the hierarchy (cardinals and bishops) to be called the "People of God."

Fifty years later we progressive Catholics are similarly excited about the leadership of Pope Francis. His widowed sister in Buenos Aires opened a window to help us visualize the ministry of her papal brother when she said, "You don't have to worry about my brother, he will have the courage to do whatever he needs to do."

History will record the similarities between Francis and John XXIII: Francis succeeded two conservative popes, John Paul II and Benedict XVI, while John XXIII succeeded Paul XI and Pius XII, two popes who also tended toward the conservative side. In one of my previous writings I predicted that Pope Francis would follow John XXIII's example and initiate Vatican Council III to bring the Catholic church into the 21st century.

Looking back now I realize that would have been a horrendous error, since the majority of the cardinals and bishops who participated would have been very conservative theologically, having been appointed by two conservative popes. Francis's decision to initiate the Vatican Synod on the Family, including choosing some cardinals and bishops whose attitude towards poor and the needy was similar to his own, was a more appropriate decision.

Sarah Durant

Sarah Durant, a popular author, broadcaster, critic and writer for Royal Academy Magazine, made some insightful comments regarding today's Church. She admits that she is a "recovering" Catholic, who remembers the relief she felt as an 11-year-old who confessed her sins to a priest in the confessional. Admiring Pope Francis she writes, "Pope Francis has made moves towards reform...but can he overcome bedrock opposition...His calls for mercy, forgiveness and a priesthood truly at the service of the laity is at the heart of a reform that, if successful, could transform the nature of Catholicism as we know it. It is as if the Church...the institution itself...is being asked to enter the confessional, acknowledging its sins, in readiness for a new start."[1]

Sarah suggests that church reform start with small steps, allowing divorced and cohabiting couples to receive communion. She argues that the Church should not judge gay men in loving relationships (both positions espoused by Francis). These changes could lead to releasing priests from mandatory celibacy and ordaining women as deacons and, in the future, ordaining women priests.

She also indirectly addresses clericalism in the priesthood: "The whole notion of an elevated priesthood and hierarchy needs addressing, encouraging more democracy and community as a way to get better shepherds for the flock." The extraordinary fact about these insights is that it comes not from a female theologian but from a recovering Catholic laywoman, who adds "If these changes come I might be tempted to join (or rejoin)."[2]

Jamie L Manson

Jamie L Manson, like Sarah, another columnist and the National Catholic Reporter books editor, received her master's degree at Yale Divinity School where she studied Catholic Theology and Sexual Ethics. She loves the Church and, like many of us, is concerned that many young Catholics are no longer attending Sunday mass or participating in receiving the sacraments. She contrasts her mother's background growing up in a Catholic community, what she calls "a village" in Queens, New York, to her own growing up as an individual with an emphasis on individual rights versus the village community values that her mother experienced.

She sees her growth as a young Catholic woman to be a radical departure from her mother's experience. In her mother's village in Queens the Church survived on community. When a young couple had a baby, the community expected them to take the baby to the local Catholic church to be baptized. When the baby became a seven-year-old, he or she attended catechism classes and made their first communion with their class, dressed appropriately to receive the body and blood of Christ for the first time. It was celebrated as a solemn event in the community.

During her mother's childhood, people communicated primarily by conversing with their neighbor. When Jamie was a teenager she and her colleagues communicated via cell phones, texting one another or sending emails on their computers. The village's community values were replaced by individual rights and practices. While Jamie's mom and dad continued to attend mass weekly and receive forgiveness for their sins monthly, those practices were no longer deemed necessary by the teenagers of Jamie's generation. Parents of teenagers no longer forced them to attend Sunday mass. Their friends played basketball or baseball on Sunday mornings. There wasn't any church community to attract their participation. Thus, what are we supposed to conclude about women's changing relationship with the Church?

Allow me to demonstrate how easily it is to create community at a parish level. I taught, socialized with and counseled teenagers during my early years in the priesthood (1960-79), I felt ready to take on the challenge of creating community for the teenagers in St. Vincent Martyr, Parish in Madison, New Jersey, when I was appointed pastor in August 1979. During the first few weekends I noticed that there weren't too many young people attending mass. Because of my training as a marriage and family therapist I knew that the last motivation I should use to encourage them to attend was to tell them they committed a mortal sin every time they missed mass on a Sunday or holy day of obligation.

To begin my positive approach, I interviewed the young religious education director and asked her how many teenagers attended the weekly religious education classes she organized. She replied about 30 students weekly. I knew that with a membership of 1,800 families in the parish those students probably represented one tenth of the total

Catholic teenage population in Madison.

I learned early in my service as a young priest in an inner city parish, Saint Agnes in Paterson, New Jersey (1960-1966), that young teenagers long for community. In order to attract them to attend weekly religious instructions and Sunday mass I created a social entertainment program called Catholic Youth Organization (CYO). I hired young local musicians to provide music so that the teenagers who attended religious education classes in the classrooms upstairs could come downstairs to the school auditorium and dance for an hour or two, before going home to get ready for school the next morning. The program was very successful due to the volunteers who taught the religious classes from 7:00 to 8:00 p.m. on Monday evenings and the volunteers who moderated the social and dancing from 8:00 to 9:30 p.m.

I knew that creating a similar "community" in a suburban parish (Saint Vincent's) versus an inner city parish would call for a different approach. I could not apply the same blueprint on the youth of Madison as I did in Saint Agnes Parish in Paterson. I decided that I should take on the role of religious education teacher for a few weeks. I planned to meet these 30 students the following Sunday. I was determined that they would participate with me in creating a community called "St. Vincent's Youth Ministry."

I invited the religious education director to sit in on the class which was held on Sunday evening at 7:00 p.m. There were about 20 students in the classroom when I entered at about 6:50 p.m. They looked very surprised to see the "new" pastor sitting at the teacher's desk. I was sure that my predecessor, Monsignor Puma, didn't focus on building community among the teenagers of the parish; otherwise there would have been more students present that evening. While waiting for the late stragglers to come along I went around and asked each student's name. I made sure to look relaxed, as first impressions are frequently lasting impressions.

At about 7:10 p.m. I walked casually to the blackboard , picked up the chalk and wrote the word SEX in large letters in the middle of the board. Several students giggled. As I paused, looking relaxed, a student in the front row spoke up. I remember his name was Hugh. He blurted out, "Father you are a priest, you don't know anything about sex." A few students snickered. I walked over to Hugh's desk and addressed him, "Hugh, please stand up." As he did so I slipped into his seat and announced, "Students, Hugh is going to take the class this evening." The whole class roared with laughter. I didn't embarrass Hugh too much. I got up after a couple of minutes and let the not-too-shy Hugh sit down. Addressing the whole class and pointing to the blackboard I asked, "Where did the word 'sex' come from?" Nobody raised a hand. I then asked, "Who created sex?"

After a moment's silence, a blond girl named Christine raised her hand and said, "I believe God created sex."

"You are absolutely correct, Christine." Next question, "When a married couple makes love and has a baby, how would you describe that act in their relationship with God?" There was absolute silence in the room. I didn't mind challenging them. I felt I had all 30 of them engaged in a theological discussion. I told them that God speaks God's words in all of creation and many theologians teach that all of us are called to be co-creators with God.

I realized that I was talking a little above their heads. "Let me give an example of how all of you can become co-creators with me of a program for all the teenagers in St. Vincent's Parish. Let's call it 'St. Vincent's Youth Ministry.' You may ask me why you can't do it yourself."

Once again Christine raised her hand and said, "Father Corr, you are not a teenager. We teenagers need to tell you what we want the program to be like along with what you want in the program." And I said, "That is correct, Christine. Let's discuss it next week and invite all your friends to come."

We had 60 teenagers, including Hugh and Christine, in attendance the following Sunday as well as two adult supervisors who would take my place moderating the program. Over the next six months St. Vincent's Youth ministry grew to 300 participants. They organized their own liturgy to be held in church each Sunday at 5:00 p.m. They attended weekend retreats called SEARCH, where teenagers gave the talks, and they participated in inter-parish basketball tournaments. One and a half years later we hired a full-time trained youth minister.[3]

Returning to Pope Francis and his attempt to create community and dialogue at the Vatican Synod on the Family. Francis addressed the Synod Fathers on October 24, 2015 as the Synod concluded, thanking them for attending and requesting they bring the message of the Synod back to the part of the world where God had called them to minister to his people. The 94 proposals presented to the Synod Fathers passed by a two-thirds majority vote and were presented to the Holy Father.

Francis said that the Synod was not about settling issues but rather about attempting to discuss issues in the light of the Gospels and the Church's tradition of 2,000 years. It was about interpreting reality through God's eyes. Referring back to Vatican Council II, Francis said the "Church spoke about enculturation as the intimate transformation of authentic cultural value through its integration into Christianity and the taking root of Christianity in the various human cultures."[3]

The Holy Father said that many delegates felt the working of the Holy Spirit, who is "the real protagonist and guide of the Synod."[4] To conclude the Synod, he said, is to return to our true "journey together" in bringing to every part of the world, every diocese, every community and every situation the light of the Gospel, the embrace of the Church and the support of God's mercy.

As the Synod concluded, 12 of my "brother" priests in my homeland of Ireland rebelled against the "systemic oppression of women within the Catholic church."

In a statement issued on November 1, 2015, the priests warned that the current "strict prohibition" on discussing the question of women's ordination has failed to silence the majority of the Catholic faithful. Father Roy Donovan, one of the priests who signed the petition, criticized the church hierarchy's "massive fear" of women. Father Tony Flannery, who initiated the signing of the petition, said it was not just about ordaining women to the priesthood but also about giving women a role in decision making. He described denying women voting rights at the October synod as "preposterous." Father Donovan said, "The synod in Rome has shown up the huge injustice and prejudice towards women. Two hundred and seventy men and not one woman voted on matters concerning the family."[5]

CHAPTER ELEVEN

The Magdalene Women

All of Ireland was shaken in 2002 when the documentary "The Magdalene Sisters" was released. The country reeled again in 2013 when a related Irish government report revealed details. The film was the true story of "fallen" women and girls who were forced to work in Ireland's 20th century workhouse laundries. They labored for hours without wages and under conditions described as "diabolical" by Steven O'Riordan, one of the authors of *Whispering Hope: The Heart-Breaking True Story of Magdalene Women*.

These laundry workers were unmarried mothers and their daughters, women and girls who had been sexually abused, women with mental or physical disabilities who were unable to live independently and young girls who had grown up under the care of the Church and the State. As in the movie "Philomena," many Magdalene residents who gave birth in the institutions were forced to give up their babies for adoption. The laundries were "a mechanism that society, religious orders and the state came up with to try and get rid of people deemed not to be conforming to the so-called mythical, cultural purity that was supposed to be part of Irish identity," according to Irish historian Diarmaid Ferriter.

An estimated 30,000 women were confined in these Irish institutions for several years without permission to speak to each other. In 1993 a mass grave containing 155 corpses was uncovered in the convent garden attached to one of the laundries. This discovery led to the revelations about these secret institutions.

In the 2015 book *Whispering Hope* Steven O'Riordan wrote:

> *"...I discovered that a developer had bought the site of a former Magdalene laundry in Dublin's High Park, back in 1993, and had permission to exhume 133 bodies...Once the exhumation started, they stumbled on 22 more bodies and had to apply for another exhumation license, which was issued by the Department of the Environment. They gave permission to exhume all the human remains, which caused upset, because we will never fully know how many women's remains were in the grave. Some of the women had no death certificates and other death certificates were incomplete. Some had a broken wrist, ankle, elbow and leg bones, and one woman was exhumed without a skull..... Nobody seemed to know who the women were, or why they died at this institution."*[1]

The records for the laundries are incomplete, but for the years 1922 to 1996 there are records for almost half of the women residents. It is disappointing to report that of the 50% recorded, only 16.4% of the women went of their own free will. The others were placed in the laundries by their families, by priests or by state agencies. And the laundries never achieved their originally cited objective of reducing the number of prostitutes in Ireland.

Steven O'Riordan was highly motivated to do something to help the Magdalene women who escaped alive from the hellish laundries. With the help of a friend, he decided to interview as many of them as possible and make "The Magdalene Sisters" documentary to report on their lives after they left the laundries. To his surprise, some of the women were so institutionalized that they were unable to live independently. They were still living in institutions operated by the state and run by nuns. When O'Riordan tried to interview the inmates, the nuns refused him entry and called the local police (Gardai).

Nuns had enjoyed high esteem in Ireland when I was growing up there during the '50s and '60s. They not only served as teachers in grammar schools and high schools but were also active as nurses and administrators of hospitals throughout Ireland. That triumphal journey for the nuns hit more than a bump in the road in 2005 with the release of O'Riordan's documentary.[2]

However, many researchers have concluded the nuns do not bear the primary responsibility for the scandal. Author Tom Inglis describes the Irish church hierarchy's "Irish Civilizing Process" with definition of appropriate penalties starting in the 19th century. James Smith of Boston University found that "the historically powerful Catholic Church and the fledgling Irish Free State cooperated increasingly through the 1920s as the self-appointed guardians of the nation's moral climate."

According to Irish scholar Tiffany Manning, members of the Church clergy emerged as the thought leaders in what should be entailed in claiming "Ireland for the Irish... Members of the Catholic clergy began building up their system of institutions in order to lock up those who did not fit the mold....Almost immediately after gaining control (of the laundry system) the Catholic Church built large, elaborate buildings to house their penitent women and gave control of the laundries to various orders of nuns."

The 2013 Irish government report further revealed the state's role. At least a quarter of the women were sent directly by the State, which gave lucrative laundry contracts to the laundries without complying with the Fair Wage Clauses and in the absence of any compliance with Social Insurance obligations, and the Irish police pursued and returned girls and women who escaped.

One of the biggest lies was that the Magdalene laundries were training institutions for financially needy girls. O'Riordan tells a story about Kathleen, who was born out of wedlock in 1935. Her mother took her to one of the institutions run by the Presentation Sisters outside Tipperary Town when she was three years old.

Two years later her mom took her to live with her grandparents in Lisvernane, County Tipperary, where Kathleen's grandfather and Uncle Mike worked in their family-owned sawmill. Kathleen loved her granny from the moment they met. Her mom moved to Dublin, 120 miles away, and only came to see Kathleen once a year for a day or two.

There was no love lost between Kathleen and her mother. Her mom frequently called her a "bloody nuisance." As she grew older, Kathleen, a curious girl, would ask about her birth. Her mom replied that the past didn't need to be discussed. However, Kathleen knew that her mother was a "fallen" (i.e., unmarried) woman, which in turn meant that

Kathleen, as her daughter, was a "devil spawn." Kathleen believed that her mother, having no source of support, had to work for the sisters.

Kathleen's beloved granny didn't last too many years and died in her sleep. Kathleen was devastated when two stern-looking men in black suits arrived carrying a coffin, while two neighbor women were washing granny. Her granddad was sensitive to Kathleen and asked, "Kathleen dear, do you want to kiss your granny goodbye?" This was Kathleen's first experience of losing a person she loved so deeply.

Since women weren't allowed to participate in processing with the body to the local church, only the men of the village joined Grandpa and Uncle Mike in following the coffin for the removal. Kathleen stayed at home and joined her mother and other local women making sandwiches for the neighbors.

To Kathleen's surprise, her mom held her hand as they walked to church the next morning for the funeral mass. As the men lifted the coffin on their shoulders Kathleen tried to walk behind them into the graveyard to say goodbye to Granny. Her mother pulled her home saying, "The graveyard is no place for women."

Her mother returned to Dublin in a couple of days and Kathleen stayed with Grandpa and Uncle Mike. This was a difficult time for Kathleen, now approaching her teens and all the changes that come with puberty. Granddad gave her Granny's bed. It was tough for one young girl, mourning her granny, to sleep on a wooden planked bed with a straw mattress. Grandpa's cottage had squeaking mice and loads of beetles on the earthen floor. They scared her. She helped out, doing some of the household chores and carrying buckets of water from the village well.

69

Kathleen entered a senior class at school but didn't get along with the gray-haired teacher, Paddy Lynch. She claimed he made her life hell and thought he treated her like that because she was a bastard. Her assignment was to set up the turf and sticks in the grate and light the fire with paraffin and matches. If the fire wasn't set up in time, Paddy Lynch would criticize Kathleen all day.

Her only consolation since losing her granny was her relationship with her friend Mary. In their free time they would walk in the woods, chat and go down to the river and swim. She had a feeling that her fun days as a teenager were coming to an end.

After one of those fun outings with her friend Mary, she ran happily into the kitchen. To her surprise her mom was sitting there, unannounced and with a scowl on her face. "There you are, you need to get your things together, we're leaving. I'm taking you to Dublin with me. There is nothing here for you now. It's time you got some training." She explained that she had found a place in Dublin where Kathleen could prepare for a job.

Kathleen was very sad about leaving Grandpa, Mary and the cottage with all the fond memories of Granny. Yet, she was excited about continuing her education and finding a job.

In Dublin, Kathleen quickly discovered that the supposed training school, St. Mary's, was not the school her mother had described. During Kathleen's entrance interview, the director, Sister Fidelis, scowled at Kathleen and handed her mother a list of all the items Kathleen would need to take up residence and join the other girls at St. Mary's. Sister Fidelis asked Kathleen if she could sing, Kathleen replied, "Sure, I do."

Sister Fidelis' sole comment was "Sister Brigid will be delighted to hear that."

A week later her mom left Kathleen permanently at St. Mary's. Kathleen had no idea when she would see her mother again. Sister Fidelis whisked Kathleen up two flights of stairs to a huge dormitory and asked her to leave the small bag that contained her cotton dress, a nightgown, soap, a toothbrush and paste. Sister Fidelis gave Kathleen a pinafore, like a habit, to put on over her dress and then led her down to the ground floor.

Kathleen expected a classroom with desks and a teacher at the front. Instead they were in a room full of steam. She wanted to ask Sister Fidelis a question but couldn't see her. As the steam cleared a little, she saw a large room with 20 or 30 girls her age, some feeding wet sheets into a big machine and several others pulling and folding dried sheets.

Some of the girls looked over at the new "student" Kathleen. The lady in charge told them to get back to work and continue singing hymns. When Sister Fidelis left the room, Kathleen walked over to say hello to the other girls. Terrified, they put their hands to their lips to indicate silence. Kathleen, although surprised that talking wasn't allowed, consoled herself with the thought that singing hymns was better than working in silence.

Kathleen awoke abruptly the next morning as a bell rang. A nun entered the dormitory clapping her hands and yelling, "Out of your beds, all of you get on your knees." The sister began to pray. Kathleen joined the girls saying their morning prayers.

On her turn, she entered the bathroom, washed her face, dressed putting on her underclothes, then took off her nightgown, which caused the nun to scream, "You! You, new girl. Do you have any modesty?" Kathleen was mortified. She then combed her hair. She didn't know how she looked, as she had just learned that mirrors weren't allowed in Saint Mary's.

She joined the girls in the chapel for mass. The girls were segregated on one side of the chapel, with a section for the nuns in the middle and a third section for the laity from the neighborhood. The nuns didn't want their girls mixing or communicating with the outside world.

Kathleen was starving, waiting in line to get into the refectory. She was shocked when all she received was a small roll of bread with a pat of butter. She was frustrated, as she couldn't talk to the girls in the refectory either. Everybody ate in silence while a nun read a passage from the bible.

Kathleen was still hoping that there would be classes for her to complete her education, but the next two hours were spent scrubbing the corridors of Saint Mary's. She worked for three months in the Calendar room, where she fed wet sheets into the monstrous drier or alternated with the girls who were pulling the dry sheets and folding them for their customers.

Sister Fidelis screamed at them, calling them idiots if per chance they jammed the machines by putting in too many sheets. "Do you realize how time-wasting this is?" Adding, "Time is money girls. You must not fall behind."

Sadly, Kathleen was just one of 30,000 Irish girls and women who were incarcerated—forced to work and live like slaves when the only accusation against them was that their mothers were unwed or they themselves were the victims of sexual assault.[3]

Steven O'Riordan convinced the Irish Taoiseach (Prime Minister) Enda Kenny and the government officials in the free state of Ireland that his country owed an apology to these women. Taoiseach Kenny invited O'Riordan and several of the women survivors to come to the Dail Eireann on February 19, 2013. He listened to their stories in the presence of the Dail members. He believed their stories of suffering.

"This heartrending story of suffering and hardships," according to *Irish Times* media analyst Stephen O'Leary, "highlights the plight of women in an Ireland dominated (at that time) by the Catholic Church." [4]

Kenny promised to put a scheme of compensation in place for all the women survivors. His apology is memorable: "At the conclusion of my discussions with a group of Magdalene Women one of those present sang 'Whispering Hope.' A line from that song stays in my mind:

> *"When the dark midnight is over, watch for the breaking day.' Let me hope that this day and this debate heralds a new dawn for all those who feared that midnight might never end."*

In 2013, the Irish government promised compensation of up to 58 million euros to the survivors of the Magdalene Laundries scheme. As of August, 2014 the State had paid out 10.3 million euros to 277 survivors. [5] The Vatican and the four religious orders that ran the laundry institutions have refused to offer any compensation despite demands that they do so from the Irish government, the United Nations Committee on the Rights of the Child and the UN Committee against Torture.

CHAPTER TWELVE

Contemplative Communities Of Women

S ince women monastics outnumber men by more than two to one, it begs the question "Why don't women religious share fifty percent of the authority in the Church?" If Saint Benedict, founder of the popular and multifaceted religious order called the Benedictines in 529 AD was still around he would be challenged by a number of progressive religious women as to why he sought a balance in his order between work, prayer and study in the various communities and didn't demand the sharing of authority between male and female Benedictines. Benedict was one of the most popular founders of religious orders. When he wrote his rule book for monks living in community under the authority of an abbot, it became a blueprint for other communities. It provided a moderate path between individual zeal and formal institutionalism.[1]

The Holy Wisdom Monastery

Benedict's female communities spread throughout the world like wildfires in California. Some of the female communities progressed from observing vows of poverty, chastity and obedience, devoted to prayer, study and good works to welcoming devoted non-Catholic women to join their order as well. The Holy Wisdom Monastery located near Madison, Wisconsin became an ecumenical community with the approval of the Vatican.

This ecumenical monastery weaves prayer, hospitality, justice and respect for all of God's creation as the heart of its community's mission. Saint Benedict must be proud that his followers at the Holy Wisdom Monastery have a long history of environmental stewardship.[2] Visitors to the monastery who walk through 130 acres of land, gardens and orchards will witness the diverse ecosystem of plants, fish, animals and humans, all living in a harmonious environment. To the surprise of progressive Catholics, the local bishop, Robert Morlino of Madison, rather than being supportive of this successful ecumenical monastery apparently feels threatened. On March 7, 2015 he sent a letter to all the priests of the diocese stating:

> *"Attendance or participation at all events held at Holy Wisdom Monastery or sponsored by Holy Wisdom Monastery or the Benedictine women of Madison by the priests of the Diocese of Madison is prohibited."*

Would Bishop Morlino act so negatively toward the monastery if the inhabitants were all male monks? Since we are living in the post Vatican Council II era where the Church is defined as the "People of God," did Bishop Morlino think of discussing his problem with the priests of his diocese or the laity before he drafted the letter that he mailed to the priests on March 7, 2015?

Sister Joan Chittister, Benedictine

Sister Joan Chittister, a member of the Benedictine Sisters of Erie PA, one of the most influential religious and social leaders of our time, gave a keynote presentation at the annual Call to Action Conference in 2015. She boldly addressed her audience, realizing that she represented monastic women religious along with secular Catholic women of the United States.

"We who care about topics with deep feelings, personal experience and strong educated opinions but have no power or authority to mandate change where change is necessary; in a society of talking points, public relation managers and political spin…we cannot blame God for what we fail to do ourselves; in a country hijacked by extremists, in a Church whose vision of the future has too long been the past, where possible answers were blocked and half the population is excluded from even thinking about them."

She is not afraid to speak out and challenge the male hierarchy to share their authority with the other 50 percent of the Catholic population. She knows that she is only respecting the teaching of Vatican Council II and speaking out as a representative of the 50 percent of the "People of God" silenced by the male hierarchy like Bishop Morlino.

Discussions on this topic with my fellow writers motivated one of the non-Catholic authors to ask me, "Why is the hierarchy of your Catholic Church so scared of women?"

Chittister reminded her audience that when the Benedictine women came to the United States in 1852, they brought 1,400 years of tradition with them and they did it differently from the Benedictine women before them. These intelligent monastic women listened to voices of the public intellectuals whose needs were different from the needs of 19th century Germany.

What kind of a church would we have today if Pope Francis and the monarchical, hierarchical Church listened to voices like Sister Joan Chittister and invited members of religious orders of women, including contemplative sisters, to participate in the Church's future decisions regarding mandatory celibacy for priests, ordination of women as deacons and priests, revising outmoded laws on marriage and the awkward divisiveness between the laity and clergy. If this were to happen, one could listen to homilies on Pope Francis's recent encyclical on ministering to our heavenly Father's gift of the earth rather than anti-abortion homilies on the feast of the Holy Family that our local community in the Diocese of Venice, Florida, was presented with at a recent mass.

Andre Louf, Cistercian

This chapter would not be complete without including a guide to our readers, male and female, who wish to enter the school of contemplation. You don't have to be a professed sister in a contemplative order or an ordained cleric to enjoy and accept the fruits of contemplation. Andre Louf, the deceased abbot (2010) of the Trappist-Cistercian abbey du Mont-des Cats in northern France, describes in his books the Cistercian way, *Teach Us to Pray: Learning a Little About Prayer* by Andre Louf and H. Hoskyns. He is erudite, personal, scholarly and speaks from the heart. He tells us that the desert of contemplation is available to all of us. The desert is a model of church, where the prophets and Jesus meet its communal struggles and their own. It is not a place where the seeker sits peacefully amid the spiritual flowers and fruits of a "contemplation" that is really blankness and deceit.[3]

Louf writes that the desert is a place of poverty, a place of continually stripping away of defenses where you are "separated from all and united to all" in the community. It is in the desert of ordinary life that the goal of ascetic practice comes to fruition. The contemplative discovers that s/he is in the presence of God…s/he stops and listens to God. Louf tells of a meeting with an old man of Skettis. He admired the old man's way of life and asked him how he achieved it. The old man said he was now as he had been throughout his life, "A little work, a little meditation, a little prayer and, in so far as I am able, I guard myself from thoughts and oppose those that present themselves to me. The spirit of contemplation came upon me without me knowing it."

Father John Main, Benedictine

Another contemplative Benedictine, Father John Main, gives a simple blueprint for a beginning contemplative:

> *"Sit down. Sit still and upright. Close your eyes lightly. Sit relaxed but alert. Silently, interiorly, begin to say a single word. We recommend the prayer phrase "Maranatha" an Aramaic word translated to either "The Lord comes" or "Come Lord." Recite it as four syllables Ma-ra-na-tha. Listen to it, as you say it gently and continuously. Do not imagine or think about anything spiritual or otherwise. Meditate each morning and evening between twenty and thirty minutes. Meditation is a pilgrimage to our own center, to your own heart. It takes us to deeper realms of silence. It is in this silence that we are led into the eternal silence of God."*[3]

Father Main's teaching on Christian meditation, according to Father Richard Rohr, OFM, director of the Center for Action and Contemplation in Albuquerque, NM, goes to the roots of spirituality and lays a radical foundation for social critique and social involvement. He quoted Fr. Main:

> *"The wonderful beauty of prayer is that the opening of our heart is as natural as the opening of a flower. To let a flower open and bloom, it is only necessary to let it be. So if we simply are, if we become and remain still and silent, our heart cannot but be open, the Spirit cannot but pour through into our being. It is for this we have been created."* [4]

In conclusion, meditation and contemplation are not just practiced in monasteries for religious women and monks but are now part of a worldwide outreach to a variety of countries including the U.S., Canada, the United Kingdom, Poland, Mexico and the Philippines.

Father Laurence Freeman, Benedictine

Following the death of Father John Main, Benedictine Father Laurence Freeman took on the task of promoting the Christian Meditation from his monastery in London, called the Meditatio House. The World Community began a program of Christian meditation for children in schools. In the Diocese of Townsville, Australia, all 32 Catholic schools have pioneered a program of daily meditation periods for young students ages 5-18. Research and experience indicate that children have a natural capacity for stillness and silence in meditation. The late bishop of Townsville, Michael Putney, believed that the spiritual experience is what stays with children. In his book entitled *Coming Home: A Guide to Teaching Meditation to Children,* "Young children have a great openness to the presence of God. If they are taught when they are young to be still so that their hearts can be open to the movement of the Spirit, they have a gift which will continue to bring them blessings throughout their lives."

Contemplative communities of both men and women religious are helping resolve the inequities that have existed in the Church's treatment of women through the centuries. What is needed in the Church today is for both male and female religious leaders, like Sister Joan Chittister, to take a stand and challenge the male hierarchy to accept that Catholic Church as the "People of God," which is clearly defined in the documents of Vatican Council II and that Church is going to be enriched by sharing its authority with female religious leaders like Joan Chittister. Other examples of emerging female leaders will be documented in Chapter XIII.

CHAPTER THIRTEEN

Educators,

Administrators, Politicians

ormer President of Ireland and a devoted Catholic, Mary McAleese professes that Pope Francis is a "wonderful gift to the Church" and in the same interview, with Michael Kelly, editor of the Irish Catholic, says, "I am ashamed, frankly, of my Church's failure to be a champion of gay rights and women's rights."[1]

She says "Francis's greatest legacy to the Church has been his welcoming of debate after the stultifying and suffocating imposed silence of his two immediate predecessors. I think Francis is allowing the church to breathe and that is a wonderful thing."

In the interview she cited numerous examples of what she considers misogyny, listing the 19th century ban on women singing in church choirs, the 1917 Code of Canon Law description of women as "objects of suspicion," to the current Vatican view that gives bishops the power to permit female altar servers, but parish priests the ultimate power to ban them.

McAleese claims that her views of Church administration and the role of women in the Church is based on the gospel and doesn't come from some weird, godless, secular world. Some people may feel that Mary McAleese is herself a gift to women in the Church. She provides a blueprint of how lay women should react to the male hierarchical Church.

Heidi Schlumpf, Professor of Communications at Aurora University, raises the question:

> *"Are women still guests in our own house?" and wonders*
> *"if women should pack their bags and find a more wel-*
> *coming home."*[2]

Schlumpf reports on a two-day conference, Women and the Church, held at Loyola University in Chicago on November 6-7, 2015. One of the presenters, Barbara Hilkert Andolsen, Professor of Applied Christian Ethics at Fordham University, proposed a question:

> *"Is active membership in the Catholic Church an exam-*
> *ple of morally serious cooperation with the evil of gender*
> *injustice?"*

She was referring to the United States bishops maintaining that the inclusion of birth control in the Affordable Care Act is material cooperation with evil. Andolsen said it is ironic, given the remoteness of the contact in the Affordable Care Act (Obamacare), compared with active participation in the sexist Church. She argued that "benevolent sexism of the Church is indeed sinful." It is not as "hostile" as the Church's attitude in the past—treating women as less than men, pointing out their spiritual weakness and their propensity toward sin. In today's Church teaching women are theoretically different from men, and the Church uses positive language, complimenting them for their role as mothers and identifying them as being more nurturing than men.

Andolsen puts closure on the discussion:

> *"The benevolent sexism of the Church is not harmless. It is detrimental to women and undermines the ability of women and their allies to mobilize and improve the situation of women."*

While the "benevolent sexism" didn't seem to affect the active mature participants at the conference, another participant, Kathleen Sprows Cummings from the University of Notre Dame, the keynote responder, noted:

> *"The alarming trend of millennial Catholic women to being less religiously devout than their male counterparts despite a long history of being religiously devout and engaged more than their male counterparts. Even more disturbing, a similar trend has not been observed among young Protestant women."*

Sister Donna Markham, OP

Sister Donna Markham, OP, Ph.D., a native of Chicago and an Adrian Dominican sister, was appointed the first female president and CEO of Catholic Charities USA on June 1, 2015. [3] She is now responsible for 65,000 employees and a budget of $53,000, 000, 63% of which comes from the government, to minister to the needs of 45 million people living in poverty, 20% of whom are children. When asked in an interview by Melanie West from the *Wall Street Journal* where women fit into the Roman Catholic Church her response was much more positive than what was verbalized by Schlumpf, Andolsen or Cummings.

She said, "I'm in very good company with Sister Carol Keehan, president of the Catholic Health Association of the United States, and Doctor Carolyn Woo, president of Catholic Relief Services. This is a wonderful moment for us as women leaders and it isn't insignificant."[4] She likes Pope Francis, saying

> *"His attention to women being involved in the highest of decision making in the Church has been very salutary for women to hear." The challenge will be what will happen through the various conferences of bishops to activate and actualize what Pope Francis has called the Church to do."*

Markham was very impressed that Francis chose to meet with the homeless people, immigrants and prisoners during his visit to the United States.

"His presence elevated our awareness, but his witness served as a catalyst to spark the rest of us to go and do the same," Markham said.

She met Pope Francis in Philadelphia and thanked him for raising the awareness of poor people across the world. She also thanked him for healing the pain of the United States sisters who faced criticism from the Congregation for the Doctrine of the Faith. Francis replied, "The sisters are doing wonderful work; keep moving forward, be courageous."

Sister Carol Keehan, DC

Sister Carol Keehan, a member of the Daughters of Charity of Saint Vincent de Paul, is the president and CEO of the Catholic Health Association (CHA) of the USA. She made headlines on June 11, 2015, when President Obama addressed the CHA.

Looking at Sister Carol he smiled and said, "I don't know if this appropriate but I just told Sister Carol I love her." He continued, "We would not have gotten the Affordable Care Act (ACA) done had it not been for her." He went on to compliment the CHA, telling them "Without your commitment to compassionate care, without your moral force we would not have succeeded."

Since President Obama's election in 2008, Keehan has campaigned with the White House to create a national health plan for the millions of individuals and families who couldn't afford insurance. During the following two years, what became known as Obamacare was created. In 2012, it was revealed that this historical program would force religious orders to provide insurance covering contraception and abortifacients for its members and employees. The bishops of the United States opposed the law vehemently and criticized ACA and Sister Keehan for supporting the Affordable Care Act. Keehan informed the White House about the bishops' attitudes, which in turn led to the president conferring privately with Keehan, regarding a proposed revision of the ACA, dispensing religious communities. Keehan approved the revision and later announced publicly, "The Catholic Health Association is very pleased with the White House announcement that a resolution has been reached that protects the religious liberty and conscience rights of Catholic Institutions."

Thanks to President Obama (and Sister Carol Keehan!) the ACA has proven to be a financial windfall for the hospital industry, wiping out nearly six billion dollars in uncompensated care, because of more paying patients. Millions of families who lacked medical insurance can now relax and enjoy their lives, knowing they can use Obamacare for their medical and emergency needs. [5]

While Sister Carol Keehan has many critics among conservative Catholics who believe that nuns shouldn't challenge or confront the United States bishops, Keehan is a

good example of what is needed in the Church today,
namely religious women taking a stand and demanding
that, according to the dictates of Vatican Council II, they
are entitled to share in decisions regarding Church admin-
istration with the male hierarchy.

Sister Carmen Sammut

Sister Carmen Sammut, a native of Malta and a missionary sister of Our Lady of Africa, has been recently elected president of the International Union of Superior Generals (UISG). She sought, without success, to be invited to attend the Vatican Synod on the family in October 2014; however, she and two companions were invited to attend Synod in October 2015 as non-voting members. The three sisters were excited, as they had an opportunity to meet Pope Francis. The UISG, which dates back to Vatican Council II, meets in full assembly every three years, bringing together top superiors of international women's religious communities. Midway between these meetings its Council of Delegates meets, usually in Rome. The UISG serves as a platform for sharing and planning global activities. The UISG is different from other international religious organizations in that new areas of the Catholic world like Africa and Asia have become active in recent years.

One hundred and twenty-five delegates, representing religious communities all over the world, attended the meeting during October 2015, just after the Synod concluded.

Sister Carmen addressed them passionately:

"We are surrounded by wealth and masses go hungry; we
are trying at all costs to prolong life and yet destroying life

in many ways. While we advance human dignity and freedom in the world, enormous numbers are becoming victims of modern slavery caused by unjust systems such as human trafficking...I ask you please to look at the signs of the times...the paradoxes which make us aware that a great part of our contemporaries are crying out to God......We, members of religious communities and families, are called to listen to God's own desires and make them our own." [6]

She quoted Pope Francis, "Go out to (the) margins to build the Church, be eccentric leaders, contemplate, as that takes us out of ourselves." Sister Carmen concluded, "We are called to be servant leaders, known for our ability to listen and see God in all things and all things in God."[7]

CHAPTER FOURTEEN

Who Changed The Face of Catholic Theology Forever?

A ccording to Thomas C. Fox, Professor Catherine Osborne of Notre Dame University liked to show a photo taken in 1946 to the students in her introductory theology class. She said, "I'd show a photo of the Founding Dinner of the Catholic Theological Society of America in 1946…and I would ask the students to "tell me what they noticed about the people attending the dinner. It is not a hard question."

Sister Mary Madeleva Wolff

The students were quick to respond. They noticed every person in the photo was male, was white and was wearing a Roman collar.

Osborne would then say, "That was the face of theology until Holy Cross Sister Mary Madeleva Wolff, then the president of Saint Mary's College at Notre Dame, established the first graduate theology school for women. Until that event took place at the School of Sacred Theology at St. Mary's, women had been excluded from the theological profession.

Osborne told the students that Wolff's intention was to increase the educational level of religious sisters teaching in Catholic schools. "But the school's very existence was so radical it ended up laying the groundwork for the first generation of academically trained Catholic women theologians in the world."

The Wolff story reveals the ingenuity, persistence and vision of a pioneering nun. It is also a testament to education and the possibilities of what religious women can do to change the institution of a Church that is literally dying today. Since the male hierarchy has chosen to protect the "good name" of the Church versus reporting pedophile priests to civil authorities and, in the opinion of some of my fellow writers on Cape Cod, the same male hierarchy are scared to share authority with significant religious women like Sister Mary Madeleva.

The story began when Madeleva, baptized Mary Evaline and known as Eva, was born, the middle child of three to August, a Lutheran, and Lucy, a devout Catholic, on May 24, 1887, in Cumberland, Wisconsin. Her father had emigrated to the United States from Germany as a nine-year-old, not knowing a word of English. Her mother, Lucy, was born in the United States, the daughter of immigrants from Germany.

Eva enjoyed her childhood with her older brother Fred and younger brother Werner, growing up in the lake district with the beautiful scenery and wildlife of northern Wisconsin. Eva absorbed her parents' complementary and sometimes contradictory qualities: her father's light touch and capacity for play, along with a humble, childlike charm and sweet gentleness, contrasted with her mother's shrewd intelligence, steely determination and profound reserve. Lucy was an exceptionally motivated mother and, like many German immigrants, worked hard and ran a strict household without any of today's amenities like electricity, washing machines, microwave ovens or refrigerators.

Eva and her brothers didn't have the privilege of attending a Catholic school. The three children received Catechism lessons from the parish priest when he was available and, if not, their mother taught them and prepared them to receive their First Holy Communion. Because of Lucy's motivation, Eva did extremely well, attending the local public school and proceeding to high school a year ahead of schedule. Eva reported the following in her memoir, (1959):

> *"Our high school offered two programs, one preparatory for college, the other terminal. As a preparation for college, we studied four years of Latin, two of German, Algebra, plane and solid Geometry, English, Physical Geography, Botany, history and Constitutional Government."*

Always the smallest and youngest in her class, Eva performed well, keeping up with the best. She graduated high school in 1904 at age 17 with seven other graduates in her class.

Since her brother, Fred was attending college at the University of Wisconsin, the family didn't have enough money to send Eva to college at the same time. She stayed home, helping her mom and assisting her dad in his workshop where he made harnesses for horses and furniture for people's homes. The rest of the time she spent reading and socializing with her former high school classmates. She admitted she was a voracious reader, especially when history books were made available to her by her mother.

By the fall of 1905 Eva was ready to do what was not a common practice for young women in the early years of the 20th century. She registered to join her older brother as a student at the University of Wisconsin at Madison. Eva's parents always valued education and were ready to make sacrifices to finance her tuition and boarding fees. The classes she took had a tremendous effect on her later writing, her teaching and administration. She signed up for classes in English, German, French and her favorite, Medieval History with its culture, guilds and architecture.

Something extraordinary happened during the school year—she became fascinated with an article in *McClure's Magazine* about Saint Mary's College. She said to herself "If this makes a difference in my life, I shall always remember it" (Wolff 1959). She applied for admission at Saint Mary's and was accepted in September, 1906 as a sophomore. As the carriage took her up the driveway to the college, she saw for the first time a Sister of the Holy Cross, whose congregation administered the college. Eva was not crazy about the strict rules that the Congregation brought with them from the French boarding school i.e. uniforms, limited visitors, limited letter writing and other practices that religious congregations of that day observed.

Eva's sophomore classes included more French, German, Logic and Christian Doctrine. She exclaimed years later that it was the sophomore English class that opened her up to a brand new world. The professor was a graduate of Harvard and a published poet, Sister Rita Heffernan. This experience introduced Eva to her lifelong love of poetry and "a manner of writing she had never tried or been taught before" (Wolff 1959). To her surprise, Eva's writings appeared regularly in the department's publication. Because of her talents in English, after graduation she was invited to be the head of the department in the academy section of the College.

In 1908, as she was entering her senior year at Saint Mary's, she decided to enter the Congregation of the Sisters of the Holy Cross, a community founded in France in 1841. Four sisters from that community came to the United States in 1843 to serve at Notre Dame. Eva received the religious name of Madeleva, at her formal reception into the community. Madeleva is a combination of Magdalene and Eva. Before she took her first profession of vows in 1910, she received her Bachelor of Arts (BA) and continued writing prose and poetry.

Her successful journey continued when she was chosen to study for her masters at the University of Notre Dame. She looked forward to being in the English department with her beloved Sister Rita Heffernan, but it wasn't to be, as Sister Rita succumbed to cancer before Madeleva made her profession of vows in 1910. Madeleva pronounced her final vows in 1914, and four years later was appointed head of the English Department at the University of Notre Dame. As expected, she received her Master's Degree from Notre Dame in 1918.

Her professional career continued to advance during the next few years as she kept on teaching, finding time for professional writing, reaching out to other poets and writers, and inviting some of them to address the faculty and students.

Unexpectedly, Madeleva's next mission became her happiest assignment. She was sent to serve as principal and teacher at Sacred Heart Academy in Ogden, Utah. This Academy emphasized the arts, especially speech and drama. Her love of the mountains and the physical beauty of the countryside inspired her to write more poetry. This assignment was followed by an appointment at the University of California at Berkeley. She entered the doctoral program as her Congregation gave her one more assignment, to be principal and teacher at Holy Rosary Academy in Woodland Hills, California.

The pressure she encountered fulfilling all these assignments finally got to Madeleva. Her superior in the Congregation realized that she had taken advantage of Madeleva's dedication to teaching and willingness to take on numerous assignments, so she offered her a sabbatical in the fall of 1933 to go study at Oxford University in England. Madeleva accepted the offer and felt honored to study medieval poetry with the internationally recognized poet C.S. Lewis. While on sabbatical, she toured Italy and made a visit to the Vatican.

Madeleva demonstrated outstanding leadership in Catholic education during her tenure as president of Saint Mary's from 1934 to 1941. She encouraged both faculty and students to make the most of their lives and their stewardship. She urged her faculty to participate in professional organizations, to attend educational meetings, to submit papers and publish wherever possible (just as she had done as a teacher since she received her Master's degree in 1918.)

She also found time to speak, write and publish. She addressed ecumenical groups of Christians and Jews and later addressed a Mormon group at the bishop's residence in Salt Lake City. She told her audiences that "the essence of our college is not its buildings, its endowment fund, its enrollment or even its faculty; the essence is the teaching of the truth." She still wrote at least one poem per month.

Madeleva had already served as president of Saint Mary's for nine years and had a new library built for the college, raising the required cash by soliciting donations from the alumnae and ignoring the criticism she received regarding women religious being fundraisers. The highlight of the first nine years occurred on March 23, 1943 when President Wolff, now age 56, suddenly realized the flagrancy of the sisters being asked to teach religion in Catholic institutions across the nation, while being denied taking courses in higher theology at Catholic universities. She shared her dilemma with several local educators, and they asked her to head a subcommittee to resolve the issue. She contacted four midwestern Catholic universities and asked them if they would admit women to their theology programs. The answer was NO! She reached out to the Catholic University of America and again the answer was NO.

Rebuffed but not vanquished, Madaleva reported her "complete failure" to Bishop Edwin V. O'Hara, the chair of the Bishops Conference of Christian Doctrine. He encouraged her to begin a theology program at Saint Mary's, for the first time open to women. She decided to go for it but found it was a challenge. She resolved to find a faculty before announcing its establishment. Three priests volunteered, including two Jesuits, to initially anchor the program. In spite of the challenge, it took her only a few months to get the program started. The new school of theology, open to female students, held its first class on June 19, 1943.

Madeleva was innovative opening a theology program for female students along with male students. Her imagination reached out to make Saint Mary's college an integrated community. At the beginning of the school year in 1941, without consultation and acting on moral impulse, she moved to admit the first African American student into Saint Mary's College. Some alumnae were furious and told her that as a northerner she didn't know what she was doing. She simply ignored the criticism.

Church historians tell us that Sister M. Madeleva Wolff still matters fifty years after her death. Her obituary published in 1964, describes her as "the most renowned nun in the world." The *New York Times* noted her wide-ranging achievements as a poet, essayist, scholar, educator and particularly for establishing the first of its kind theology program that accepted female students along with laymen. While history records her leadership and contributions to American Catholicism and solidified her place among 20th century women, we ask if she had lived and served in the post Vatican II era would she have corralled her fellow religious women to challenge the male hierarchy to share authority in the Church with them, as the dictates of Vatican Council command?

The Body Soliloquies

Who speaks of bridal bed and nuptial splendor

Waiting the royal bedroom and his spouse

These cannot match the innocent couch I tender

The King who comes to rest within my house

O Blessed nothingness, whence I am able

A little bed, a little chair, a table

A candles halo in the shining gloom

There should be flowers, where the King reposes

With subtle fragrance to beguile his rest

I place his bridal lilies, bridal roses

My while, unfolded self upon His breast.

Sister M. Madaleva Wolff

CHAPTER FIFTEEN

The U.S. Bishops' Response to a Progressive-Minded Pope

May 2015 *The New York Times* journalist Frank Bruni wrote, "Pope Francis fashioned himself as a feminist last week" (5.6.15). Bruni reported how thankful he is for this Pope, how he admires him greatly and believes that a change of tone, even without a change of teaching, has meaning and warrants celebration.

However, Bruni added that "a change of tone in defiance of fact should be flagged as such." Bruni was referring to Francis's reported outrage at society's failure to ensure that women receive equal pay for equal work, a situation that Francis decried as a "pure scandal." Bruni didn't stop there, writing "Francis left out the part about women in the Roman Catholic Church not even getting a shot at equal work. Pay isn't the primary issue when you're barred from certain positions and profoundly under represented in others."

The question will be asked by Catholic historians in the next century, if not already, whether Pope John Paul II's edict in 1994 that forbade women's ordination cemented the Church's tradition of exalting men over women and whether the continued symbolism, rituals and vocabulary that confirm this inequality was necessary or merely what always was must always be.

Bruni challenges us, "For all the remarkable service the Church performs, it is one of the world's dominant and most unshakeable patriarchies with tenets that don't abet equality." What if Pope Francis challenged Pope John Paul II's non-infallible edict on the grounds that it was not infallible and could be challenged. Would the United States bishops support him?

The answer is probably NO! Here in the United States, when President Obama proposed the Affordable Care Act (ACA), he was reportedly motivated to do so by Sister Carol Keehan, president and CEO of the Catholic Hospital Association. U.S. bishops had lobbied strenuously against the ACA's requirement that employers include contraception in workers' health insurance. The bishops' concern was that the rule applied to employers from religious schools and hospitals. The bishops opposed the rule even though only a very small minority of American Catholics accept the Church's prohibition against artificial birth control.

From the earliest days of his pontificate, Francis' words "have been rich in language of movement and change, of his wish for a Church unencumbered by old attitudes and habits, moving beyond the confines of church structures into the streets"[1] (Tom Roberts, NCR 12.4.17, 2015).

When Francis addressed the National Council of the Italian Church a week before the United States bishops met in Baltimore for their annual meeting in November 2015, he exhorted the members not to place ultimate trust in structures, organizations and laws but to embrace a Church that is forever changing.

During the 50-minute exhortation he emphasized how integral change is part of the healthy life of the Church.

Progressive thinkers in the Church will say that it is too bad Pope Francis didn't give the same exhortation to the United States bishops before they began their annual meeting in Baltimore. According to journalist Tom Roberts, the United States bishops are not responding positively to Francis's exhortation to accept change. Roberts reported that the bishops spent most of their time during the four-day conference reviewing old documents that were retreads of previous documents, e.g., condemnation of pornography.[2]

During the bishops' conference, one outside observer noted that "a lack of engagement by the bishops with Francis's vision is a 'disconnect' between the bishops and ordinary Catholics." A Catholic historian who observed the conference interpreted the reluctance of the United States bishops to accept the tone and priorities of the current papacy as a signal that the American hierarchy mistrusts Francis' vision.

Bishop Robert McElroy of San Diego created some melodrama by proposing to his colleagues that they scrap the old statement regarding forming a conscience for faithful citizenship and refashion a position that places concern for the poor and the environment at the core of Catholic social teaching.

> "If I understand Pope Francis correctly," said McElroy "the issue of poverty, particularly global poverty, with all of its victimization of men and women across the world, and children, the global poverty and degradation of the earth, which threaten the whole of our humanity, that these two issues are at the very center of Catholic social

teaching as priorities for us in every public policy decision. These issues are not presented in this document…Keeping to the structure of the worldview of 2007 tilts the document in favor of abortion and euthanasia and excludes poverty and the environment.” [3]

Clearly annoyed, the conservative Galveston-Houston Cardinal Daniel DiNardo shot back as expected, quoting the pope (Benedict XVI) who appointed him. Stressing the need for fidelity to Sacred Tradition of the pre-Vatican II Church, DiNardo said, “Ours is a hermeneutic of continuity here, bishop.” He angrily continued: “I believe we read (the Pope) correctly and have responded with real attentiveness to the pastoral ministry and magisterium of Pope Francis, though perhaps not to your satisfaction” nor with “the rhetorical flourish which you bring them.” [4]

According to Michele Dillon, professor of sociology at the University of New Hampshire, “That the bishops continue to highlight the same issues…abortion, same-sex marriage and religious freedom …demonstrates a disconnect with the language and concerns of ordinary Catholics….The world has changed since 2007” says Dillon, who has done extensive research on the state of the Church in recent decades. She says the United States bishops are not addressing the issues of the Church's growing Hispanic population, the environment, and the increasing poverty in the United States. Dillon believes that the United States bishops are “increasingly out of touch with the day-to-day concerns of Catholics and the wider culture.”[5]

Pope Francis wants dialogue, which is why he had two Vatican synods on the family—one in 2014 and one in 2015. The United States bishops don't dialogue with Francis. Most of them were chosen during the papacies of John Paul II and Benedict XVI. They were ordained bishops because of their conservative theological tendencies and they still follow the dictates of those two popes.

These bishops appear to have given mere lip service to Francis's appeal to embrace change at the synods. Instead, they focused on the document "Create in Me a Clean Heart: A Pastoral Reponse to Pornography," and its corrosive effects on the individual and on society. Francis urged them to delay their debate of the document until their annual conference back in the United States The bishops' intense focus on "Create," a document of only 34 pages, caused several journalists attending the conference to laugh among themselves, with one gentleman saying "We're pretty sure they are against porn." [6]

What does the future hold for the United States bishops? Church historian Massimo Faggioli, director of the Institute for Catholicism and Citizenship at the University of St. Thomas in St. Paul, Minnesota, says:

> *"What is necessary is a regime change, and that may take a quite a few years. The discontinuity of old practices and debates about abortion, same-sex marriages, religious freedom and sex must end. If we don't continue the development of our social teaching, ministering to our environment, God's gift to all mankind the Church will cease to be relevant to today's educated Catholics. Otherwise we are waiting until Francis's episcopal appointments tip the scale in a new direction of dialogue."[7]*

According to Faggioli, Pope Francis is diminishing the role of the Curia, increasing the number of female employees at the Vatican, and counting on the Church to be more synodal in the future. A regime change is necessary, as the clear resistance by the United States bishops indicates that "they are not convinced that Francis's vision for the Church is something they can trust and believe in." The bishops are not comfortable with the practice "of thinking and speaking freely." They use "continuity" as a very convenient shield that protects them. However, while the bishops are preoccupied with their own self-protection, who is protecting and building a future for the United States Church?

CHAPTER SIXTEEN

A Baptist President Advocates For Women

ormer President Carter wrote an inspiring and overwhelming book, published in March 2014, entitled *A Call to Action: Women, Religion, Violence, and Power.* While some may question Carter's legacy as our president, nobody will dare challenge his advocacy for women and his lifetime ministry to wipe out injustice to women in religion, in civil society and in the remote villages in jungles where the Carter Center sponsors programs to ameliorate the horrible living conditions of women and their families.

In December, 2009, he was invited and accepted the invitation to speak at the Parliament of World Religions, an audience of several thousand assembled in Australia, regarding the global scourge of gender abuse. He told his audience that "my remarks represent the personal views of a Christian layman, a Bible teacher for more than 70 years and a former politician." One of his many insightful comments was "while we citizens of the world are guided by Universal Declarations of Human Rights, the Bible, and the Koran, some selected scriptures are interpreted, almost exclusively by powerful male leaders within the Christian,

Jewish, Muslim, Hindu, Buddhist and other faiths, to proclaim the lower status of women and girls."

Carter was obviously including the male Catholic hierarchy of the Catholic Church under the heading of "powerful male leaders" who interpret the scriptures for both male and female members.

Carter's claim that this misinterpretation of scripture, i.e., that women are inferior to men, spread to the secular world, which in turn justified acts of discrimination and violence against women e.g., unpunished rape, sexual abuse and worldwide trafficking of women and girls.

Zainah Anwar, founder of Sisters in Islam, Malaysia asks,

> *"If women are equal in the eyes of God, why are they not equal in the eyes of men?"*[2]

Carter reminded his readers that the *Universal Declaration of Human Rights* was ratified in 1948 by a vote of 48 to 0 with 8 abstentions. Eight Islamic governments voted in favor of the declaration. The consequences of world wars and polarization within regions and individual countries make it impossible for the same commitments to be made today.

It is helpful to examine the Declaration to understand the universal commitment to the equal status between men and women, no matter what career they pursued:

> PREAMBLE. Whereas recognition of the inherent dignity and of equal and inalienable rights of all members of the human family is the foundation of freedom, justice and peace in the world.

Article 1. All human beings are born free and equal in dignity and rights.

Article 16. Men and women of full age, without any limitation due to race, nationality or religion, have the right to marry and found a family. They are entitled to equal rights as to marriage, during marriage and at its dissolution.

(2) Marriage shall be entered into only with a free and full consent of the intending spouses.

Article 23. (2) Everyone, without any discrimination, has the right to equal pay for equal work.

President Carter emphasized that these were clear and unequivocal commitments made by our world leaders in 1948. It is shameful that these solemn international agreements later ratified by national legislative bodies are being violated so blatantly. It must be presumed that many of the world's religious leaders, who remained remarkably silent, did then and always would exempt themselves and their compliant followers from the granting of these guaranteed equal rights to women and girls.

Rev. Dr. Susan Brooks, former president of Chicago Theological Seminary wrote:

"War and violence against women not only have similar social, cultural, and religious supports, they are mutually reinforcing. These supports allow societies to tolerate conditions in which a third of women and girls can be treated

violently, without mass outcry and rebellion. When we challenge the attitudes and norms that enable violence against women we are helping confront the conditions that support war." [2]

Carter admits that while Christian churches argue about the status of homosexuals, the use of contraceptives in marriage, when, if ever, abortion is permissible, one of the most prevalent and divisive issues is "whether or not women are equal to men in the eyes of God." Obviously Carter believes they are, and when the Southern Baptist Convention decided in 2000 to exclude women from serving the church as deacons, pastors or chaplains in the Armed Forces or even as professors in some Convention seminaries, both he and his wife Rosalyn decided to end their relationship with the Convention after he had been a member for over 70 years.[3] He proudly reports that in his local Maranatha Baptist Church "we enjoy having both men and women pastors, and at this time half of our elected deacons are women."

Carter continued:

"There is one incontrovertible fact concerning the relationship between Jesus Christ and women: he treated them equal to men, which was dramatically different from the prevailing custom of the times. The four gospels were written by men, but they never reported any instance of Jesus condoning sexual discrimination or the implied subservience or inferiority of women. In a departure from earlier genealogies, Matthew even includes four gentle women (all of whom had extramarital affairs) among the connections of Christ: Tamar, Rahab, Ruth,

and Bathsheba. The exaltation of and later devotion to Mary, Jesus' mother, is a vivid indication of the special status of women in Christian theology."

There are several incidents reported in the scriptures where Jesus ignored the strict prohibition of a Jewish man dealing with women in public. He had no hesitancy conversing at the community well with a Samaritan woman who was a pariah among the Jews and her peers because of her ethnicity and lascivious behavior. She accepted him as the promised messiah and took his message back to her village, the first example of an evangelical witness.

Jesus also rejected the double standard of punishment for adultery by granting pardon and forgiveness to a guilty and condemned woman.

Dr. Alison Boden, Dean of Religious Life, Princeton University wrote:

> *"The Gospel of Jesus Christ has as its center the end of domination of every kind. For some Christians to use the Gospel to compromise the human rights of women and others borders on the obscene. Propagated with appeals to idealized heritage, immutable sacred history, and paternalistic care of the religiously ignorant, their rights-denying actions must be exposed for what they are—formal policies for the retention and augmenting of power by those men who already have it. The ethic of Jesus Christ proclaims the radical equality men and women. The ending of the subordination of women—and all who are dominated—is critical to the building of the reign of God on earth as it is in heaven."* [4]

109

Readers may wonder if today's male Catholic hierarchy remembers that women travelled with Jesus' entourage and their spiritual and financial support within ministry was accepted. Does the same hierarchy remember Mary, the sister of Martha and Lazarus, who Jesus visited often in Bethany and who seemed to be among the few people who knew Jesus would be crucified and would rise again from the dead? The same Mary also anointed Jesus' feet with perfume a few days before his crucifixion. Then Mary Magdalene, one of his loyal followers, visited the empty tomb and Jesus appeared to her and instructed her to tell the apostles and other disciples, who were hiding in a secret place, that he, Jesus our savior, had risen from the tomb.

Some Scripture scholars claim that Saint Paul's letters to the early churches contained a bias against women when he directs them to worship with their heads covered, keep their hair unbraided, dress modestly and never adorn themselves or speak at a worship service.

In response to the apparent disharmony between Jesus and Saint Paul, President Carter reminds us of Paul's letter to the Galatians which states, "But now that faith has come, we are no longer subject to a disciplinarian. for in Christ Jesus you are all children of God through faith… There is no longer Jew or Greek, there is no longer slave or free, there is no longer male or female, for all of you are one in Christ Jesus" (Gal. 3:25-28).

Saint Paul thanked 28 outstanding leaders of the early churches, at least 10 of whom were women. "I commend to you our sister Phoebe, a deacon of the Church at Cenchreae….Greet Priscilla and Aquila, who work with me in Christ Jesus…Greet Mary who has worked very hard among you…Greet Andronicus and Junia, my relatives who were in prison with me; They are prominent among the apostles and they were in Christ before I was…Greet Philologus, Julia, Nereus and his sister, and Olympas, and all the saints who are with them" (Romans 16:1-7).

Carter said,

> *"It is inconceivable to me that Paul would encourage and congratulate inspired women who were successful dea-cons, apostles, ministers and saints and still be quoted by male chauvinists as a biblical source for excluding women from accepting God's will to serve others in the name of Christ."*

The question been raised today by reform-minded Catholics who seek the ordination of women is (since according to the testimony of Saint Paul there were female apostles, deacons and female saints who served with Jesus in the early Church), why did Pope John Paul II issue his Ordinatio Sacerdotalis (May 22, 1994) to the Catholic bishops of the world, stating:

> *"Priestly ordination, which hands on the office of teach-ing, sanctifying and governing the faithful, has from the very beginning been reserved to men alone. This tradition has been maintained by the Oriental Churches."*

Some historians claim that Cardinal Ratzinger, the head of the Congregation of the Faith at that time, encouraged Pope John Paul II to write the proclamation denying qualified Catholic women the right to become ordained priests.

President Carter asks a similar question regarding female members in the Baptist Church. "The question is whether we evangelical believers in Christ want to abandon HIS example and exclude a vast array of potential female partners who are equally devout in responding to God's call to ministry."

In light of how Jesus treated women, and being a Jew himself, the patriarchy in the Catholic Church needs to examine its attitude towards the role of women in the Church in light of Saint Paul's letter to the Corinthians. "You need to learn however that woman is not different to man and man is not different to woman and both come from God" (1 Cor. 11:11-12).

CHAPTER SEVENTEEN

Authentic Feminine Authority Needed in the Church Today

T he average Catholic believes that as long as women are banned from ordination to the priesthood and thus have no hierarchical position, they have no ecclesiastical authority. Pope John Paul II definitively affirmed the Church's ban on women priests in his 1994 Apostolic letter *Ordinatio Sacerdotalis*: "the Church has no authority whatsoever to confer priestly ordination on women and this judgment is to be definitively held by all the faithful."

Theologian and professor at Madonna College in Livonia Michigan, Monica Migliorino Miller, disagrees with the opinion of the majority of Catholics, while admitting "The Church has been in a state of crisis over the role of women for a very long time. She writes in *The Authority of Women in the Catholic Church* published in 2015, "What is desperately needed is a true theology of feminine authority - indeed a true Catholic Feminism."

Miller quotes Pope Francis, who called for such a theology in his September 30, 2013 *America* magazine interview:

113

"We must therefore investigate further the role of women in the Church. We have to work harder to develop a profound theology of the woman. Only by making this step will it be possible to better reflect on their function within the Church. The feminine genius is needed wherever we make important decisions. The challenge today is this: to think about the specific place of women in those places where the authority of the Church is exercised for various areas of the Church."

While the Bishops of the United States failed to pass a controversial pastoral statement on the role of women, which had been on their agenda for nine years, soon afterwards Archbishop Rembert Weakland, OSB, the retired bishop of Milwaukee and sympathetic to the ordination of women, told an audience of women at Trinity College that the debate over women's role in the Church and society "is not over, it is just beginning."

Unfortunately, there are thousands of young Catholics, the majority of them women, living both here in the United States and in my native Ireland, who have given up the practice of their faith and refuse to accept Pope Francis's message: "The feminine genius is needed wherever we make important decisions." How then, I ask, can these non-practicing Catholic women participate in resolving the crisis of faith that plagues the Catholic Church if they continue to refuse to attend weekly Sunday mass in their local parish?

Miller goes on to demonstrate how the crisis concerning the role of women in the Church profoundly affects every aspect of ecclesiastical life; i.e., sacramental, liturgical, spiritual and moral. She interprets the crisis differently than do the regular feminist theologians. She said

"Fundamentally, the crisis has to do with the meaning of authority itself," and adds "Women do possess authority in the Catholic Church." [1]

Edith Stein, the great German philosopher and Catholic martyr, stated "Woman…is called upon to embody in her highest and purest development the essence of the Church…to be its symbol.[2] Miller claims that the authority of women is different from the authority exercised by the Catholic ordained priesthood. It is an authority that is complementary to the priesthood and it is an authority without which the sacramental life of the Church and redemption would not exist.

Professor Miller's analysis of the crisis in the Church is different from the comments and interpretations already presented in earlier chapters of this book by feminist theologians. Miller said that these theologians believe that the hierarchical structure of an all-male priestly authority is an inherently unjust system and sinful in its exclusion of women from positions of power.

Even though today's most influential feminist theologian, Elizabeth A. Johnson differs with Miller's interpretation of the Church's crisis, she still quotes her in her book, *She Who Is: The Mystery of God in Feminist Theological Discourse*:

"Even as I write, women in the Catholic community are excluded from full participation in the sacramental system, from ecclesial centers of significant decision making, from law making and symbol making and from official public leadership roles, whether in governance or liturgical assembly. They are called to honor a male savior, sent by a male God, whose legitimate representatives can only be male, all

of which places their persons precisely as female in a peripheral role...In a word, women occupy a marginal place in the official life of the Church; that is, necessarily there but of restricted value." [3]

Johnson's claim differs from Miller's when she states that the only way for women to achieve recognition and power in the Church is to be associated with the power of God himself and believes that the feminine role is less valued when compared to men, especially male priests.

Conversely, Miller emphasizes the present value of women in the Church and how Christians understand the order of redemption and how salvation is actually communicated to the world. Both authors agree that the crisis troubles the faith life of Christians, particularly in their participation in reception of the sacraments and in the areas of morality.

Miller describes authority as the power to give life and the responsibility to oversee the good for that life. God is the source of life. He has created us. It is obedience to God our creator that gives us life. Bound up with God's creative will is the beauty and also the horror of human freedom. The same God who created us contains the mystery of the Blessed Trinity, which we don't understand but yet believe because it is contained in the Scriptures, i.e., God the Father begets the Son, and the Holy Spirit proceeds from the Father and the Son.

Authority, according to Professor Miller, if it has any basis in the truth of the oneness and plurality of the Trinity, is not one single thing. God himself is not a single automotive thing, without relations and neither is the Church and the authority that functions within her, authority that functions within her, authority exists in a Covenant - indeed, in a free dialogue between Christ and the People of God, i.e. the Church.

Just as God the Father created us, so also does his Son Jesus Christ create something other than Himself. He creates us – his Church – the people baptized into his body, i.e., the People of God. To understand our relationship as members of the Church with Christ our founder, it is best to compare our covenant with Christ to the covenant of marriage.

> *"The authority of this new covenant is not only the authority of the bishops and priests, an authority held by men, who through Holy Orders stand in the place of Christ. The New Covenant is a marital union between Christ and the Church, so the meaning of Church authority is marital. In 1976 the Vatican issued a document called Inter Insigniores or a declaration of the question of admission of women to the ministerial priesthood."*[4]

It teaches that the covenant, even from the Old Testament times, had a nuptial character. The Chosen People are the spouse of God.

The Sacred Congregation for the Doctrine of the Faith admitting women to the ministerial priesthood (1976) was followed by Vatican Council II, Vol. 2: More Post Conciliar Documents by Austin Flannery, O.P.:

> *"From his pierced side will be born the Church, as Eve was born from Adam's side. At that time there is fully and eternally accomplished the nuptial mystery proclaimed and hymned in the Old Testament: Christ is the bridegroom; the Church is his Bride whom he loves because he gained her by his blood and made her glorious, holy and without blemish and henceforth is inseparable from her."* [5]

Miller continues to create a distinction between the feminists' view of the Church's crisis and their negative attitude towards a male priesthood. She has written that feminist theology is struggling to find a symbol of redeemed humanity, but not even Jesus is adequate for the task! Miller's teaching on redemption is that is neither male or female centered - it is covenantal. Androcentrism and gynocentrism both fail to explain the equal dignity of men and women. (Androcentrism is placing the masculine point of view at the center of one's world view. Gynocentrism is placing the feminine point of view at the center.)

Miller writes that radical feminists reject Christ as the sole model for redeemed humanity because his masculinity enforces male dominance. She herself says that the redemption is not mediated by a male Christ alone, but by the Christ, and the Church redemption through the covenant. Christ is the model and source of redemption only in union with his "bride" the Church.

CHAPTER EIGHTEEN

Women Deacons and Women Pastoral Life Directors

P ope Francis has made it clear that he wants bishops to make courageous proposals to address the shortage of clergy throughout the Catholic world. One of the participants at the Vatican Synod on the Family, Canadian Archbishop Paul-Andre Durocher, took Francis's suggestion to heart. During his three-minute address to the Synod in 2015 he proposed three courses of action, the third related to women. He proposed the establishment of a process that could eventually give Catholic women access to ordained deacons. He told the Synod that "it is not a closed issue. There has been no dogmatic statement saying that women cannot be ordained" (to the diaconate).[1]

As frequently happens, there were negative responses. William Ditewig, a deacon of the Monterey Diocese, CA and a professor at Santa Clara University said, "Admitting divorced and remarried Catholics to Communion should take precedence over ordaining women to the diaconate."

Phyllis Zagano, an internationally acclaimed Catholic scholar and lecturer on contemporary spirituality and women's issues in the Church, wrote it is a healthy sign for the Church to discuss the question of women deacons in the Church. "There has never been any definitive ruling against the earlier tradition of ordaining women to the deaconate." [2]

Now that the topic has been brought up, Zagano endorsed the Canadian Archbishop's proposal, saying "Bishops' conferences around the world should discuss the question and send a 'dubium' (a formal question) to Rome, asking if they may ordain women to the diaconate"

On August 2, 2016, American scholar Phyllis Zagano, was named by Pope Francis to a Commission to Study the Women's Diaconate. Members of the committee include: Spanish Sister Nuria Calduch-Benages of the Missionary Daughters of the Holy Family of Nazareth, Italian professors Francesca Coccini and Michelina Tenaci, Italian Sister Mary Malone of the Franciscan Sisters of Blessed Angela of Foligno, and German professor Marianne Schlosser.

Phyllis Zagano wrote in Harvard Divinity Bulletin, "Ordain Catholic Women as Deacons."

Recognizing that all persons, including women, are made in the image and likeness of God—actually a staple of Catholic teaching—does not automatically grant women access to priesthood. Even given the abandonment of the iconic argument (some still say it is "implied" in the 1994 document) there is the question of authority, supported by the assertion that the ban on women priests is of divine law. Hence the specter of women priests cannot really be raised with the ordination of women deacons.

Comparing the Catholic Church in the United States to the Church in South America, she said that not every bishops' conference in the United States wants female deacons, but in South America there are bishops who say they would ordain women as deacons in a minute.

Chicago Archbishop Blase Cupich, also a delegate at the Synod, responded to a television interview and said that he had not kept up with the topic but was "always willing to read and be informed." Ditewig added, "Some see ordaining women as deacons as the beginning of the slippery slope to ordaining women as priests." Zagano responded with:

> *"The fact of the matter is that the diaconate is not the priesthood. It is a separate and complete ministry. If the hierarchy of the Church can understand the separation and distinction between the two, that's a long way to restoring women to the diaconate. I think the Holy Father understands that."*

We all know, that from the beginning, Pope Francis called for a wider inclusion of women in the life and ministry of the Church. Zagano reminds us that if he wants to include women in the governance and ministry then the obvious way is to restore women to the diaconate, and in doing so he will also make them clerics of the Catholic Church.

According to Father Luke Hansen, an associate at *America* (2012-2014), lay people who support the ordination of women to the diaconate should, as a first step, make their conviction known to their local priest or diocesan bishop. The second step would involve the bishops, who are familiar with the pastoral needs of their dioceses and the gifts of their lay people. If the bishops believe that God is calling women to serve as deacons, they should pass on this conviction to the National Conference of Catholic Bishops or to Pope Francis directly. As we have noted already, Francis wants bishops to make courageous proposals to address the shortage of clergy in their dioceses. Zagano supports this proposal and adds that while plenty of women are engaged in Church ministry, ordaining them as deacons would make their work an extension of the bishop's ministry.

Bishop George Murry of Youngstown, Ohio said:

> *"Women are involved in a variety of ways in the Church, but are women in decision-making roles? That is where we have to move from talking about inclusion to acting on it." He said, it would be "a wise idea to look into it, learn more about it, and then to present a proposal to the Pope to say either there are theological problems or not; and, if not; if not move forward."* [3]

The magazine *Crux* reported in the March 7, 2016 edition that Saint Pius X Catholic Church of the Archdiocese of Baltimore, situated in the town of Rodgers Forge, is not just talking about sharing the ministry with women, they are acting on it. A 63-year-old woman, Carol Pacione, has taken over the role of the senior official of the parish because they don't have a full-time priest. She fulfills most of the non-spiritual functions of a pastor. She counsels engaged couples in preparation for their marriage, manages contractors, organizes capital campaigns, and decorates the altar with flowers for the Sunday liturgy.

According to Jonathan Pitts of the Baltimore Sun (3.7.16), Pacione is a pastoral life director, one of a small group of lay leaders who enjoy all the powers and responsibilities of a traditional parish priest, except for the ability to offer up the Eucharist or administer the sacraments. Pacione is a pioneer among women who have assumed some of the highest leadership positions in the church and in Catholic Churches of the United States, according to Sean Caine, Vice Chancellor of the Archdiocese of Baltimore. Such an opportunity was made possible by the Second Vatican Council (1962-1965), it redefined the Church as the "People of God" and declared that it isn't just ordained priests who carry the gift of ministry but all men and women baptized as members of the Catholic Church. The revision, Canon 517-2, loosened the strictures on who can lead parishes.

Today there are about 35,000 "lay ecclesial ministers"—many known as pastoral associates—working full time in Catholic Churches in the United States. According to Dr. Thomas Groome, director of the Church in the 21st Century Center,

> *"without them, pastoral ministries would be crippled. This is the cutting edge of a deep shift in how the Catholic Church conducts its formal ministries, away from a purely clerical paradigm to a more inclusive and representative one."* [4]

Pacione is a graduate of Loyola University and is one of 431 such lay people who serve as pastoral life directors in the United States. She has three colleagues who serve in the same capacity in the Archdiocese of Baltimore. Prior to accepting the position of pastoral life director from Cardinal Keeler in 2002, Pacione had served as director of youth ministry at her home parish, director of the Family Life Bureau for the Archdiocese, and was working as a pastoral associate at the Church of the Nativity in Timonium where she led a $1.8 million campaign for renovations to the sanctuary. The Reverend Louis Reitz, who had served as associate pastor at St Pius for several years before Pacione took over in 2002, said members and even staff at the parish were "probably a little resistant" to their new leader at first, but her determination to include the parishioners and staff in every major decision won the community over. [5]

Appointing Catholic women as pastoral life directors of parishes is a giant step towards sharing authority in church ministry with women. What is a surprise to students of Church history, like myself, is that it happened because of the revision of Canon Law—the rules that govern the day-to-day life of the Church—and that it happened during the conservative papacy of Pope John Paul II. The year was 1983, when Church authorities were concerned about the aging clergy and anxious to implement the resolutions and attitudes of Vatican Council II and thus to bring the Catholic Church into closer alignment with the modern world.

Kerry Robinson, executive director of the National Leadership Roundtable on Church Management, commenting on Canon 517-2, said it turned a potential crisis into an opportunity. Being able to hire professionals, both men and women, from outside the traditional seminary pipeline brings positive energy to the weakened Church. Up until then, Church authorities tended to look only to the ordained—to men for these administrative skills in a parish.

> *"We were probably overlooking hidden assets in our faith communities, the expertise and talents of the lay faithful. Now we look much more to laymen and women."*[5] *Canon 517-2 reads should a "dearth of priests" occur, a bishop could "entrust"…the exercise of pastoral care of a parish to a deacon or some other person who is not a priest so long as such leadership takes place under the supervision of a priest.*

Throughout the world bishops may hire and appoint men and women of faith, with backgrounds in finance, business management, counseling, education and more to serve as parish life directors under the direction of a local priest. The only problem experienced so far, according to Mary Gautier, a senior research associate at The Center for Applied Research on the Apostolate at Georgetown University (CARA), is in some very rural parishes in Alaska and Montana, where it is difficult to find suitable candidates for the role of parish life directors.

The Official Catholic Directory 2015 indicates that the shortfall between the number of active diocesan priests and the number of parishes in the United States remains entrenched, despite 515 new ordinations in 2014. There are 16,462 active diocesan priests and 17,324 parishes. Thus, there are currently 862 more parishes than active diocesan priests. You would have to go back more than a decade, to 2004, to find a year in which the total number of these clergy was larger than the number of parishes.

Carol Pacione says the model works well at St. Pius X parish. The community of 1,300 families calls on priests from Loyola University in Maryland, from local parishes as well as retired and semi-retired priests in the area to fill in.

Pacione says, "We have been blessed, the priests who help out have become members of our faith community in their own right. You would never know we don't have a pastor."[6]

As presented in my last chapter, Dr. Monica Miller says Catholic women do share authority with men in the administration of the Church. The appointment of 431 pastoral life directors to oversee parishes proves that Miller's statement is accurate. Gautier reports the

Center she is associated with experiences just one problem—the attitude of some bishops. While the number of lay ministers has doubled since 1990, the smaller number of pastoral life ministers has remained essentially flat. Students of Church administration and development may say there are bishops who are scared to allow women to manage big parishes and prefer to ask priests to cover more than one parish, import foreign priests who speak poor English or even close parishes.

Aspiring lay ministers can now pursue formal coursework at many Catholic institutions, including the Ecumenical Institute at St. Mary's Seminary and University in Baltimore. Both Cardinal William H. Keeler of Baltimore and his successor Archbishop William E. Lori, both early proponents for the pastoral life directors, have given prominent roles to women in the Archdiocese. Barbara McGraw Edmondson serves as superintendent of schools and Diane L. Barr serves as chancellor for the Archdiocese, which means she is their head lawyer.

"The Church has settled on the priesthood, but there are already many women in executive and other higher level positions," according to Caine.

> *"Our job," she maintains, "is to make them more visible, so that young girls and young women can see and recognize it and take it into account" when weighing career options or how to serve the Church." [7]*

Carol Pacione served at the helm as pastoral life director at St. Pius X parish in Rodgers Forge for 13 years and became a model for women church leaders in the Archdiocese of Baltimore. Her determination to involve the parishioners in all major decisions set a standard of how a woman's strength and ingenuity can not only crack the glass plated ceiling of the Catholic Church's denying ordination to women, but open up the Church hierarchy to share church administration with the other 50% of the human race, i.e., WOMEN.

CHAPTER NINETEEN

The Forgotten Heroines of Ireland

G rowing up in Ireland in the '40s and '50s I was very conscious of my father's desire that all 32 counties in Ireland would become a free independent state, liberated from British colonial rule. My dad, John Francis Corr, was too young to serve as a volunteer in the Easter Rising of 1916. However, he did become a volunteer in support of Eamon DeValera a couple of years later, thus participating in the Civil War that followed from 1919 to 1922.

The Easter Rising happened at the General Post Office (GPO) on O'Connell Street, Dublin, in 1916. I remember Master McCarthy, our teacher and principal at Legaginney National School, telling us during our history class in 1948 that the Irish rebels were under the command of Padraig Pearse, a school teacher by trade and a highly respected leader. McCarthy outlined the rationale for the timing of the Rising, stating that England, an ally of Russia, France and Serbia was already at war with Germany, Austria and Hungary. The War, which began on July 28,1914 and ended on November 11, 1918, was called the Great War or the First World War. According to several of today's historians, the War was caused by misconceptions and several misunderstandings. One misunderstanding was that Germany never expected England to join the War against them, believing they were too preoccupied with the Irish rebellion. 17 million died and 20 million were wounded during the World War. The Irish rebels mistakenly misjudged the British government's desire to maintain control of Ireland.

Master McCarthy never told us that Irish women participated in the Easter Rising. We also did not learn about the brave nurse Elizabeth O'Farrell who volunteered on April 29, 1916 to take commander Padraig Pearse's message of surrender from 15 Moore Street Dublin through the bullet-riddled streets across town to the British military outpost.

According to an article by journalist in the *New York Times* of March 18, 2016, 260 women participated in the Rising and only Constance Markievicz, a school teacher turned sniper, made it into the history books. Not until the Centenary Celebration in 2016 did two female historians, Mary McAuliffe and Liz Gillis, unearth a wealth of information about the 77 women who were imprisoned for their role in the Rising. The research by McAuliffe and Gillis revealed those 260 women were not just committed Irish nationalists, but were also long time campaigners for social justice, fighting inequality on multiple fronts: land reform, labor battles and women's suffrage. They wanted to create a society in Ireland where they would have an equal say with men in the governance of Ireland. They strongly believed that the republic they chose to fight for was the surest means to that end.

On a speaking tour in 1917, historian Margaret Ward declared that Ireland did something very unique in 1916 to advance equality between the sexes, "That wouldn't have happened without the efforts of women before the Rising." [1] Johanna Sheehy Skeffington (1877-1946) a founding member of the Irish Women's Union, a suffragette and Irish nationalist told her audiences that "it is the only incidence I know in history when men fighting for freedom voluntarily included women."[2]

The progressive leanings of the Easter Rising leaders were evident in the language of the *Proclamation of an Irish Republic* read aloud by Padraig Pearse on the steps of the GPO. He addressed "Irishmen and Irishwomen" guaranteeing "equal rights and equal opportunities to all its citizens."[3] Because this happened at a time when women in most of the world had yet to secure the right to vote, this guarantee was no trivial thing.

As Master McCarthy taught us, it took over six days for the British troops to quell the rebellion. Sixteen rebel leaders including Pearse and the movement's greatest champion for equality, the socialist leader James Connolly, were executed. It took six more years and more bloodshed before Ireland won a limited independence for 26 of the 32 counties.

Women's activism expanded rapidly during the following tumultuous six years. The Women's Parliamentary Organization, "Cumann na Mban" in Gaelic, grew from 1,700 members in 1916 to 20,000 in 1921. While I was still a teenager, my mom Nell told me she had been a member and all she was asked to do during the Civil War was to transport ammunition in our horse and trap from one barracks to another. She said she felt very safe fulfilling this assignment, as the British soldiers would never suspect that she, a woman, had ammunition hidden in the trap.

The human rights language didn't make its way into the 1922 Irish Constitution. Padraig Pearse couldn't enforce it, since he had already been executed. Irish women over 21 years old received full voting rights. The hierarchy of the Catholic Church in Ireland had great influence over the new democracy of the free state, resulting in women being excluded from sitting on juries. In 1932, a marriage ban forced women who worked as teachers or civil servants to retire upon their getting married. The 1935 Conditions of Employment limited women's ability to work in industry.

It was the 1937 Constitution drafted under the leadership of Prime Minister Eamon DeValera that sealed the women's fate in Ireland for decades. I was disappointed to learn that, as my dad was a devoted DeValera fan. I expected that "Dev," being born in the U.S., would be as progressive as Padraig Pearse. While Pearse welcomed women to serve in the Easter Rising, DeValera refused to allow them to join his battalion at Boland's Mill outpost in 1916. Dev was the only leader to refuse women's participation in the Rising.

Article 41 of the Constitution reads "By her life in the home, woman gives to the state a support without which the common good cannot be achieved." DeValera closed the door on women's progress in Ireland just as much as the Church hierarchy did by supporting Pope John Paul II's decision to deny ordination to the priesthood to women forever.

With the Centenary Celebration of the Easter Rising now happening in Ireland and the erasure of its first wave of feminism, a new one is surging, propelled in part by the commemorations of the Rising. When the national theater of Ireland, the Abbey, released its centenary lineup of plays, all but one were written by men, and an "Estrogen Rising" erupted. The ensuing furor highlighted women's under representation in Irish theater, film, media and politics. Unfortunately, the nuns in Ireland didn't join the Estrogen Rising. They were probably still recovering from the negative press they experienced following the revelation by thousands of young girls who had suffered tremendously in the Magdalene Laundries managed by nuns over a 200-year period.

The most recent surge of feminism in Ireland became very real when reproductive activists struck a new note of militancy, chaining themselves to the pillars of the GPO to protest a 1983 constitutional amendment that equates the right to life of the unborn with the right to life of the mother. In imitation of the Easter Rising 100 years earlier, these women dressed as suffragists and read aloud their version of the 1916 Proclamation. They declared the "right of all people in Ireland to ownership of their own bodies."

In the same streets where Elizabeth Farrell walked through gunfire some 100 years earlier, these modern day activists forged a link between their struggles and the unfulfilled hopes of their sisters from another era. As I stated earlier, one of the ongoing trials for Catholic women today both in Ireland and in the United States is to share authority with male priests at the parish level and with the male hierarchy worldwide. Catholic feminists like Rosemary Radford Reuther, Elizabeth Schüssler Fiorenza and Sister Elizabeth Johnson deal with the struggle more like the female suffragists in Ireland in April 2015; whereas Dr. Monica Miller, an author and Professor of Systematic Theology at Madonna College in Livonia, Michigan says,

> *"It is clear that authority, whether male or female, cannot be reduced to sheer possession of power for the sake of*

dominating the direction or order of the group. Authority is not an extrinsic organizational force. The authority of the covenant of redemption is certainly not this. When we talk of the authority of Christ the Head, and His Bride the Church we are really speaking at the edge of mystery. Covenantal authority is the basis of creation and redemption and must be live as mystery….a living and understanding that is only possible through grace."

"The greatest spiritual danger for the Church that will collapse her covenantal authority is the desire of women to destroy or possess what man has. When women do this, they deny and forfeit their own dignity and responsibility. This is, of course, the essence of the push for female priests. For the woman to own what man has will not result in simply exercising an authority that has been "reserved to him, because to destroy this authority is to destroy him."
4

I don't for one minute expect the suffragists in Ireland to follow the rationale outlined by Dr. Miller in the above paragraph. They should join the 12 Irish priests who took the same position Padraig Pearse and his followers adopted in the 1916 Proclamation, calling for equal freedom for both Irish men and women. The priests called for the Church to end the "systemic oppression of women and to institute full equality of women within the Church."5

CHAPTER TWENTY

Loretta Duquette – Lay Ecclesial Minister

Before I met Loretta, I was excitedly telling a good priest friend of mine, Father Ed, about the increasing number of lay men and women who were serving as pastoral directors of parishes in the United States, where there was a shortage of priests. He just smiled at me and said "We have such a lady in our parish, who previously served as a Lay Ecclesial Minister in a parish in Mississippi. If you wish to interview her for your book, I will have our business manager send you her name and phone number."

Lay Ecclesial Ministry is a term adopted by the United States Conference of Catholic Bishops (USCCB) to identify the relatively new category of "Ministers" in the Catholic Church, who serve the Church in parishes that don't have an ordained Catholic pastor. Simply described, they are co-workers with the bishop, along with priests and deacons in the vineyard of the Lord. Lay Ecclesial Ministers are not ordained.[1]

Prior to Vatican Council II, several ministries that had been part of

135

the priests' "job description" were returned to the laity, and several new forms of ministry emerged since John XXIII "opened up the windows" of the Catholic Church during Vatican Council II (1962-1965). Rather than defining the Church as the hierarchical monarchical structure, as it had been defined for a couple of centuries, the Council Fathers redefined the Church as the "people of God," which meant that all baptized Catholics share in the "lay apostolate" and had, in fact, a "lay vocation" to assist in evangelizing the world.

According to the USCCB this ecclesial ministry includes:

- Authorization from the hierarchy to serve publicly in a local church

- Leadership in a particular area of ministry

- Close mutual collaboration with the pastoral ministry of bishops, priests and deacons

- Other ministries assigned, i.e., human, spiritual, theological, and theological in nature [2]

As expected, some bishops feel threatened by this action of the USCCB and have noted that the creation of this new ministry does not represent a new level of the hierarchy, even though the USCCB clearly states that lay ecclesial ministers serve the Church in the same vocation as bishops, priests, deacons and theologians.

In Chapter XVIII, I presented the life and ministry of Carol Pacione, pastoral director for 13 years at St. Pius X Parish, Rodgers Forde, Baltimore, MD.

I now introduce you to a former Lay Ecclesial Minister, Loretta Duquette. She was born on October 1, 1939 in Buffalo, NY, the fourth of ten children to a very spiritual father and devout mother.

A professional colleague interviewed Loretta and described her as "a strong, smart, business-savvy, independent, adventurous, positive, engaging professional woman." I was very impressed with how she developed her spiritual life from the time she was a young girl open to guidance of her parents. She was not the usual volunteer I was used to working with as a Catholic priest in New Jersey. She enjoyed being taught by nuns in Catholic grammar school in Buffalo. She started writing poems in grammar school. She attended public school, as her parents couldn't afford to send ten children to a Catholic high school. Being an above average student, she started high school at age 12. Her dad encouraged her to take business courses, because he didn't expect her to go on to college after high school. He didn't realize Loretta's potential to receive scholarships.

Loretta got her first job as a legal secretary at a local law firm. In the meantime, she continued to grow spiritually, reading religious books.

She married at the early age of 18 and had five daughters. Although the marriage was not compatible, being a loyal Catholic, Loretta stayed in the relationship until it became totally unbearable. After 20 years, she initiated a divorce which, unfortunately, became an acrimonious process. With the help of a spiritual director, she sought and received an annulment from the Catholic Church. Eight years later, she married Jerry, a handicapped widower, whom she loved dearly until his death. Her dad, whom she also loved, died at age 52, when Loretta was still in her twenties.

She sought and obtained employment as a real estate broker/sales-person. Her girls did well in school, with tutoring provided by their mother. Loretta still had the passion to become better educated. Although she had already graduated from high school, she returned to high school at age 28 and studied subjects that she wanted to pursue. She continued her education at Mt. Saint Mary's University in Emmitsburg, MD and earned a master's degree at the Notre Dame Graduate School of Christendom in Alexandria, Virginia in 1992.

When asked during an interview if she enjoyed the college experience she replied, "It was pure joy; I loved it."

After five years in real estate and nine years as a legal secretary, she was recruited into financial services for 12 years.

Encouraged by spiritual directors, she joined the Handmaids of the Precious Blood and thoroughly enjoyed the experience of participating in the Perpetual Adoration of the Blessed Sacrament. In her daily practice of mental prayer she felt the presence of the Holy Spirit guiding her every action. The director of the community asked her to help develop the Oblate Center. She accepted the invitation as if it were coming directly from God. She worked diligently at the assignment for four months. Her commitment at the monastery came to an abrupt end when her youngest daughter Catherine died at age 31.

In 2010, Loretta found an advertisement in the Sunday Visitor newspaper, seeking applications for the position of Lay Ecclesial Minister for a parish in West Point, Mississippi. After prayerful reflection, she applied for the position, providing names of spiritual directors and other references. It was explained to her that she or whoever would be appointed to the position would be responsible to the bishop of

Jackson. The search committee at Immaculate Conception Church in West Point was impressed with Loretta's resume and references and invited her to come for an interview. The committee informed her that she was just one of the five final applicants for the position - the others were a male deacon, a nun and two other women.

The sacramental minister, Father Robert Dore, interviewed Loretta for an hour on the phone the day she called to apply for the position. Philip Dimino, the president of the Parish Council, arranged for her to fly into nearby Columbus airport, where one of the parishioners, Maureen Colorado, picked her up. Loretta reported that the interviews, which lasted through the weekend, were conducted by members of the parish council and a monsignor representing the bishop were intense. She felt relaxed during them, and she left the decision the committee would make totally in the hands of God. The Committee told her on Sunday they would notify her shortly if they decided to choose her as their lay ecclesial minister. Two weeks later Philip Dimino called and told her the Parish Council had chosen her to serve for a period of three years. Loretta gracefully accepted their offer and made plans to collect her belongings, drive to West Point and move into the rectory of Immaculate Conception Parish.

Her responsibilities at Immaculate Conception parish included

- Caring for 72 families

- Catechetical instruction of children

- Bible study for adults twice weekly

- Teaching the Confirmation and Communion classes

• Teaching RCIA...the Rite of Christian Initiation of Adults for prospective conversion to Catholicism, who are above the age for infant baptism

• Teaching marriage preparation to engaged couples

• Preparing parents for the baptism of their children

• Conducting Scripture and Communion services

• Preparing homilies, her reflections on the Gospel reading of the day

• Exposing and reposing Our Lord for Eucharistic Adoration

• Conducting Ash Wednesday service and Stations of the Cross during Lent

• Leading the recitation of the Rosary and prayers during Eucharistic Adoration

• Visiting hospitalized parishioners who are hospitalized

• Taking Holy Communion to and visiting homebound parishioners

• Attending monthly Deanery meetings with priests, Lay Ecclesial Ministers and Pastoral ministers

• Overseeing remodeling of the Parish Center

• Scheduling blood donors for the annual blood drive, thus meeting our blood donor goals

• Organizing a Parish directory, by scheduling
family pictures for the 72 individuals and families [3]

Loretta's schedule at Immaculate Conception Parish kept her very busy. She received great support from the Parish Council and volunteers from the parish regularly accompanied her as she made home visits and brought Holy Communion to the homebound.

There was just one older man who refused to accept Holy Communion from Loretta. He wasn't nasty to her, in fact he began to exchange emails with her during her stay in West Point.

When asked if there had been any negative experience during her ministry at Immaculate Conception Parish, she replied that she felt lonely living alone in the parish rectory.

One of the former parishioners at Immaculate Conception Parish, Maureen Colorado, described the community of 75 families as very traditional. They wanted to have a priest to say mass on Sunday rather than on a Saturday evening. Father Robert Dore, who drove several miles from his own parish to celebrate mass for the community of Immaculate Conception on Saturday evenings, told the Parish Council who served on the search committee that they must "widen the net" to find a lay ecclesial minister. Thus, instead of advertising in local Catholic papers they chose the Sunday Visitor and received a number of applications, which they narrowed to five to be interviewed.

Maureen commented that she was "very touched" from the moment she met Loretta at the airport. She said "Loretta breathed new life into our Parish." The search committee's concern about her being age 72 turned out to be an unfounded fear. According to Maureen,

"Loretta has the energy of 10 people."

The people of the Parish were very impressed with Loretta's deep spirituality, being that she was "deeply rooted in the tradition of the Church." The children of the parish loved her as their religious education teacher. She not only shared the Catholic faith with them at their level but also shared her spirituality with them.

Maureen summarized it best when she said, "Loretta is God's Word in action."

Those of us who regularly criticize the USCCB and worry about the future of the Catholic Church should now congratulate the United States bishops for their insight in creating the lay ecclesial ministry and pastoral director ministry. Loretta Duquette's life and ministry match the life and ministry of those of us male members of the church who have been ordained priests forever, according to the Order of Melchizedek.

CHAPTER TWENTY ONE

Where Do Religious Catholic Women Go From Here?

I began this book about women and the Church by reporting not only that women were denied equal rights as members of the Church, i.e., the people of God, but also in civil society where they received only half the pay men received for doing the same work. Betty Friedan, founder of the National Organization of Women (NOW), did research, interviewed hundreds of professional women on equal rights and sent the report to McCall's magazine, which frequently published her articles. To her surprise the male editors rejected her report, with the chief editor adding the insulting comment "Betty has gone off her rocker."

Helen Robinson, the first female United States Senator from Colorado, accused United States men of treating their wives as possessions instead of marital partners. She told the men who bragged about how they treated their wives, "Kind sirs, you are suffering from premature canonization."

Meanwhile, women religious in the United States met the Vatican's inquiry with what they christened "productive resistance." The year was 2011 when Mother Mary Clare Millea and her cohort of visitation teams made on-site visits (or audits) with all the religious communities in the U.S. who agreed to cooperate. Unfortunately, many religious communities, particularly those belonging to the Leadership Conference of Women Religious (LCWR), saw the visitations by Mother Millea and her team as an indictment of the United States sisters and a thinly veiled attempt to corral the sisters back under the control of the patriarchal hierarchy.

A second group of United States religious women, a more traditional union called the Council of Major Superiors of Women Religious (CMSWR), decided to view the visitation by Mother Millea and her team through the lens of organizational behavior—the study of organizational structures. Instead of feeling admonished by the Vatican, the sisters used the visitation to rediscover their identity as "Gospel women." CMSWR engaged with their visitors, participating in prayerful contemplation and robust communication, ultimately subverting the motives of those who originally set up the audits according to Sacred Heart Sister Jean Bartunek, who said,

> *"What the leaders of the women's congregations did was basically give a model that can be helpful for a lot of people when somebody with a lot of power is telling you that you have to do something that doesn't feel right. And that is something that is a pertinent way for other organizations beyond religious congregations."*

Research for this book revealed that a few events and circumstances caused the LCWR and some members of the CMSWR to interpret the visits organized by the Vatican Congregation as a disciplinary activity. The majority of women religious in the United States acted differently to the male hierarchy of the United States after Vatican Council II

(1962-1965). They assimilated most of the progressive decrees of the Council. Some of the more progressive communities like the Sisters of Charity of Saint Elizabeth, Convent Station, Morris County, NJ revised their community rules and gave sisters the choice of continuing to wear a habit or change to secular attire, and some sisters were given permission to live with another sister in an apartment separate from the convent. While they all continued to pray and work together, many of the younger religious women became integrated with the lay people in their local parish community.

While the majority of religious women were becoming more modernized, the majority of the male hierarchy was regressing to a pre-Vatican II mentality. Much of that regression can be attributed to the election of two conservative popes: John Paul II (1978- 2005) and Benedict XVI (2005-2013).

When Pope Paul VI was elected pontiff following the death of the progressive Pope John XXIII on June 3, 1963, he appeared at first to be moderate theologically, as he continued the Vatican Council for two more years. Pope Paul formed a commission of theologians and married couples to study the issue of married couples regulating conception.

After prayerful reflection and study, the commission reported to Pope Paul that the question of how to regulate conception should be left to the consciences of the couples. The Holy Father shocked most of the adult Catholic world when he released *Humanae Vitae* on July 25, 1968, stating that each and every act of love (intercourse) between a husband and wife must be open to the procreation of children.

As religious women continued to assimilate the Documents of Vatican Council II and integrate the teachings of Council into their ministry to the poor and downcast, they developed their own theological understanding of scripture and morality. More than 500 nuns from all over the U.S and Canada gathered in St. Louis for two days in November 2015, for the Council of Major Superiors of Women Religious symposium on religious life. This event was inspired by the Year of Consecrated Life, which was then being observed worldwide as part of Pope Francis' call to men and women religious to "wake up the world." The women attended lectures given by Archbishop Augustine Di Noia, secretary for the Congregation for the Doctrine of the Faith (CDF) on the topic, a theological exploration of the prophetic character of religious life. Other lectures from a mix of theologians, canon lawyers, authors and philosophers followed, rounding out the theme of the symposium: how women religious are specially called to share the gospel with a broken world.

One or two of the presenters were traditional in their presentations. Sister Mary Prudence Allen, an author and philosopher, criticized Immaculate Heart of Mary Sister Sandra Schneiders' well-publicized critiques of Catholic patriarchy. Allen drew gasps from the hundreds of sisters in the audience when she quoted Schneiders "that the religious hierarchical structures are demonic and satanic power structures." Allen continued her criticism, saying "She fails to distinguish between the structure itself and the poor use of structure...To me, that is a philosophical error in her thought."

Many of the religious attendees experienced a wake-up call. Sister Constance Veit reported that the symposium had given her a new understanding of the prophetic responsibility granted to women religious.[1]

The first National Sisters Week occurred earlier in the same year at St. Catherine University in St. Paul, MN, as 160 women, both lay and religious, arrived at the wintry campus on March 8th. Reportedly, this week was originally organized to record the religious sisters' stories and bring the reality of religious life to a whole new generation of young women who would then in turn consider entering a religious community.

"The overall feel of the weekend was such a joyous environment. Everyone seemed to have that in their heart. Everyone was so open and willing to talk, sharing stories," said Villanova University junior Megan Hopkins. "Having the opportunity to meet other college students who were discerning 'What's next?' was beautiful, whether that was single, married or religious life," said Enedina Maya, a student at the College of St. Rose in Albany, NY.

Sister Rosemary Nassif, director of the Conrad N. Hilton Foundation's Catholic Sisters Initiative, was delighted with the positive comments and grateful for the Hilton's donation of $3.3 million to St. Catherine University, establishing the Sister Story project to bring the sisters' stories to a wider audience.

> *"We at the Hilton Foundation have this hypothesis," Nassif said. "There is a declining number of sisters in North America. The reality that causes is complex. It has a sociological reality, religious reality, probably a Catholic reality. Young people don't know sisters and don't know about sisters' lives."* [5]

"I think that is so true" replied Caitlin Dickinson, a senior at the Felician College in New Jersey. She said she is seriously considering a religious vocation.

> *"What kick-started my search was my friend Sister Clare. So building relationships, I think, is the most important*

thing that can be done here."

The average age of sisters in the U.S. is 74. One of the older attendees at the symposium, Sister Jeanne Marie Gocha, said she was tired of hearing the same old story that our numbers are down but was excited to hear at one of the communication sessions that she and her counterparts are "sitting on gold mines" of stories. [3]

With the number of active sisters decreasing annually, the issue of caring for elderly religious women has become a challenge and, in some communities, a crisis.

Sr. Ann Veronica Burrows recalled entering religious life as a postulant in 1966: "All I thought I would be doing is teaching people about Jesus." Now at 66 years old, she has acquired a master's degree in long-term care along the way and is now at the helm, supervising a $19 million renovation of Camilla Hall, a retirement home outside Philadelphia for retired sisters of her community, the Servants of the Immaculate Heart of Mary. When Burrows entered The Immaculate Heart of Mary Community of educators, evangelists and catechists numbered 2,400.

CHAPTER TWENTY TWO

What Do We Tell Pope Francis?

F or those of us, who rejoiced at the election of Cardinal Jorge Bergoglio from Buenos Aires to the papacy on March 13, 2013, know that Pope Francis is not comfortable leading a monarchical, hierarchical Church. Throughout his public life as a pastor, bishop and cardinal he was noted for his humility, emphasis on God's mercy and his deep concern for the poor.

We who served the Catholic Church, both during Vatican Council II and afterward, know that the Fathers of the Council wanted the Church to adapt to the changes in society. As Ilia Delia reported in her book, published in 2015, *Making All Things New: Catholicity, Cosmology, Consciousness*...She reached out to Arthur Koestler to clarify her position...

"The difficulty of Vatican Council II was instituting change as a universal decision...Lessons from biology tell us, universal change is virtually impossible. In self-organizing of open systems, all change is local. An open-system cannot function as a monarchy but as a hol-

archy, which means a system composed of interacting holons."
(Koestler, 1967) [1]

What Pope Francis needs to do is to continue to hold synods in different parts of the Catholic world, encouraging and empowering local churches, to make changes that will meet the needs of local communities. According to Delio, "Local churches empowered from within, can best discern their pattern of relationships and organizations that vitalize a Christic way of life. To be "Church" in accordance with nature is to "live locally."

Observing Pope Francis's leadership style; some conservative bishops and cardinals appointed during the papacy of Pope John Paul II and Pope Benedict XVI are disappointed that Francis does not put an emphasis on condemning abortions and sins of the flesh, while many female theologians and progressive thinking Catholic women accuse Pope Francis of being all talk, with no action, when it comes to creating equal authority for women with men in the Church. Some would tell Francis that an open system church dictated by the Documents of Vatican Council II cannot function if it is a misogynist Church.

We also need tell Francis our Christian life is intended to be an open-systems life, which shares life with us fully and completely. Delio tells us:

> *"The Church is grounded in openness to God, to something "other," to newness of life. The Incarnation is deeply relational, in so far as the Divine is imbedded in materiality. Jesus was foremost about relationships and in particular the type of relationships that create wholeness and community."*[2]

Leonard Swiller wrote in 1983: "Dialogue is a conversation on a common subject between two or more persons with different views, the primary purpose of which is for each participant to learn from each other."[3]

Let us then ask Pope Francis, Bishop of Rome, to invite the College of Bishops to join him as designers, stewards and teachers of the laity. Those of us with backgrounds in parish ministry can explain to Francis how the Catholic laity, both male and female, are capable of creating patterns, where in which their capabilities to understand complexity, clarify vision, think together and learn together happens over time with support from the local bishop or pastor.

The learning process can be initiated by celebrating the different family cultures within the parish community, e.g., the families of Italian heritage can demonstrate to the rest of the community what makes the Italian family different socially, artistically and spiritually. The families of Irish heritage can use the annual celebration of Saint Patrick's Day on March 17th to share with the community, why their Irish faith in the Blessed Trinity is memorialized each year by wearing the three leaf shamrock on St. Patrick's Day and why the Irish Catholics devotion to the Blessed Virgin Mary, mother of their Savior, motivated them to create a special name for her i.e., "Muire".

While Pope Francis inspires the "whole" to take responsibility for the "whole Church," we lay members of the Church are called to join leaders as co-teachers "who empower a vision of the whole."

> *"This type of Catholicity is needed today, a renewal of life energies, inspiring a rise in consciousness and empowering participation in creating a whole earth community —peace among people and justice with nature...around the globe"[4]*

Pope Francis needs to change his perception of women religious, in particular from seeing them simply as mothers and sisters, to recognizing them for what they are, intelligent professionals. Francis needs to realize that the LCWR (The Leadership Conference of Women Religious) in particular…have assimilated the Documents of Vatican Council II and have subsequently progressed theologically, spiritually and sociologically, while the male hierarchy in general have failed to keep the promises of the progressive resolutions, adopted during Vatican Council II. There is evidence that many of the men have regressed back to the conservative ideologies of Pope John Paul II and Pope Benedict XVI. A good example is Cardinal Gerhard Ludwig Muller, Prefect of the Congregation for the Doctrine of the Faith, who continues to defend the indissolubility of Marriage and denies divorced and remarried Catholics the right to receive Holy Communion, even though Pope Francis is considering removing the ban and encouraged priests to resolve the issue in the Internal Forum, because divorced and remarried Catholics are not excommunicated.[5]

Another example is Archbishop Wojciech Polak, Poland's Catholic Primate and chief pastor of 15 million Catholic Poles living in the United States and elswhere. In an interview reported in the *National Catholic Reporter*, Polak said, "As in every country, our Church has to know how best to proclaim its good news to contemporary people… Here in Poland we have a particular duty to recall the legacy of Saint John Paul II, apply it to the to the social and moral projects of the current times." That undimmed loyalty to John Paul was showcased at the Vatican Synod on the Family, during October, 2015, when Archbishop Polak said, " I think God had given us a Pope for a specific time, who is able to speak in contemporary language about today's key issues… but we are also counting on him not to stray from the positions of Pope

John Paul and to understand the pastoral realities."(and then the confession) "We have to adjust his teachings to suit our pastoral programs. [6] Archbishop Polak was determined to follow the decrees of the deceased Pope John Paul II, rather than respecting the present Pope's wishes.

From his election to the Papacy in 2013, Pope Francis has had to face curial headwinds, as he attempted to introduce structural reform at all levels, according Hans Kung, Swiss citizen, Professor Emeritus of Ecumenical Theology at Tubingen University in Germany. Dr. Kung said" He specifically advocates structural reforms…namely decentralization towards local dioceses and commmunities, reform of the papal office, upgrading the laity, against excessive clericalism and in favor of a more effective presence of women in the Church, above all, in the decision-making bodies. And he comes out clearly in favor of ecumenism and interreligious dialogue with Judaism and Islam."[7]

Kung who was a classmate of Cardinal Ratzinger, who later became Pope Benedict XVI, was not popular with popes because of his outspoken criticism of Papal Infallibility and individuals, who they perceived to be harmful to the faithful, who were struggling to retain their practice of their Catholic faith.

> Kung wrote that the negative response by Archbishop Gerhard Muller, prefect of the Congregation for the Doctrine of the Faith, written as a document in the *L'Osservatore Romano* on October 23, 2013, affirming the exclusion of remarried divorced Catholics from the sacraments. King said,
>
> *"It was precisely the reactionary strategy of the doctrinal Congregation that led to the Church crisis and triggered the*

153

exit of millions of Catholics from Church, particularly those who were divorced and remarried, as they were excluded from the sacraments." [8]

In addressing Pope Francis and sharing our feelings about what he needs to do to reform and save our Church in crisis, we ask "What kind of reformer is Francis?" Church historian and Jesuit Fr. John O'Malley told the *National Catholic Reporter* on October 17, 2013, "With Francis there is no mincing of words. You know where he stands, and you can't give it a spin. He takes seriously the mission of the Church: a new mission that is really old and the most fundamental mission of the Church to be love among all, patient and full of mercy to all."[9]

O'Malley said it is significant that since Francis did not participate in Vatican Council II, he is free to create a mission for the post-Vatican II Church. Some examples of Francis's attitude were announcing himself as bishop of Rome, versus "Holy Father." Instead of washing the feet of a male Catholic on Holy Thursday, he washed the feet of a Muslim woman. He called eight cardinals from different parts of the world to begin working on structural reform within the Vatican and the worldwide church.[10]

While these actions by Francis are classified progressive, other actions are disappointing, and drive the discussion to ask whether the present Pope is a true reformer. On the one hand Francis is not going to ordain women or marry a gay couple during his tenure as our Pope. An editorial in the National Catholic Reporter stated, "His attitude towards women seems woefully outdated, calling them "strawberries on the cake." Despite his words about including them in the Church, he has yet to involve them in any substantial way in church governance."[11]

Author Austen Ivereigh, who dared to title his masterful biography of Francis *The Great Reformer*, gave an insightful analysis of what we are experiencing.." Just as the Church in Spain and Italy was the source of the Counter-Reformation, and the Church of France and Germany the source for the Second Vatican Council, Latin America is now the wellspring of for a new era of church reform."[12]

Francis perplexes many Catholics in Europe and North America, who want to label him liberal or conservative. Ivereigh said this is happening because Francis uses a lens and language that comes from outside those categories.[13]

Since Francis was comfortable visiting people in the slums of Buenos Aires, that we in the United States would be uncomfortable doing. When he recently visited a poor community in Rome, he instructed the leaders to avoid telling people where they were wrong, but to "get closer" to the people, walking with them and respecting their needs. His recently published encyclical 'Laudato Si', reminded us that we are all connected to the earth; all minerals, plants, animals, people, all parts of the universe, that exist beyond our knowledge, are all gifts from the almighty creator. Each person on the planet is called to care for that universe.

While thanking the Holy Spirit for the gift of Pope Francis, let us pray for him…

> *Almighty and eternal God, bless and protect Francis, with good health and stamina as he continues to reform the hierarchical monarchical church, respects planet earth, reaching out to the victims of pedophile priests and to all women in the Church, especially religious women. If it is*

E P I L O G U E

R esearching this book was both a challenge and a blessing. A lifelong Catholic who served in the priesthood for 28 years, I believed I would learn nothing new about the role of women in the Church. I thought that the conflict between the Church's male hierarchy and women religious was something that began less than 50 years ago…WRONG. I also thought that none of the leadership positions in the international Church organizations were headed by a woman…WRONG.

The hostility between the male hierarchy and women religious in the Church actually began a century before Vatican Council II (1962-1965). On the issue of women's leadership in the Church, Wall-Street Journal reporter John J. Fialka, author of *Sisters: Catholic Nuns and the Making of America*, tells their story and passionately analyzes their remarkable contributions to education, healthcare, social reform, civil rights, and their patient but determined persistence of a meaningful role in the Church.

Today, with Catholic women religious and Catholic lay women becoming leaders of international Church organizations, there is a renewed promise for women sharing equal authority with men in the future Church. As reported in chapter thirteen, Sister Donna Markham, OP, Ph.D., was appointed the first female president and CEO of Catholic Charities U.S.A. This Dominican sister supervised a staff of 70,000 employees and administered social services to 10 million people at a time when, according to Crux Magazine, Pope Francis was pushing to give women more prominent roles in the Catholic Church.

Sister Carol Keehan, a powerful Daughter of Charity of Saint Vincent de Paul, was named the most powerful person in Health Care in 2007. Prior to that article Sister Carol had been chosen as President and CEO of the Catholic Health Association (CHA), a position she still holds.

As President and CEO of Catholic Relief Services (CRS), Doctor Carolyn Woo, a third Catholic female leader, supervises a staff providing services to 100 million people who are poor, hungry and displaced. Carolyn was one of five presenters in Rome at the release of Pope Francis's encyclical on the environment, Laudato Si (Praise Be).

While representing CRS, Carolyn was featured in the May/June 2013 issue of Foreign Policy, as one of the 500 most powerful people on the planet and one of only 33 listed in a force for good. Her faith journey and work at CRS are recorded in her book Working for a Better World, published in 2015 by Our Sunday Visitor.

Many Catholic readers feel that the male hierarchy of the Church is afraid of women religious and don't want to see them ordained as either priests or deacons. I, however, feel that since the election of Pope Francis in 2013, a new revolution, spearheaded by the women religious leaders themselves, is taking place.

Sister Anne E. Patrick, Professor Emerita of Religion and Liberal Arts at Carleton College in Northfield, Minn. and past president of the Catholic Theological Society of America brings a scholar's thoroughness and a spiritual woman's passion to the changing landscape of women's vocations. Dr. Patrick received the John Courtney Murray award in 2013, the highest honor bestowed by the Catholic Theological Society of America on a member who has achieved a lifetime of distinguished theological scholarship. In receiving the award, Patrick concluded her acceptance with an unusual word of thanks - to the "mostly white men" who "encouraged my participation and leadership when white women were under-represented in the society."

In her book, Dr. Patrick notes the difference between how the Church hierarchy treated nuns 50 years ago and how the National Assembly of Women Religious (NAWR) is vocal on Social Justice and changes in the Church. Groups like The Green Sisters and Nuns on the Bus now set their own agendas. Patrick reported that women of mature, committed lives in justice-oriented communities who make their own decisions scare Vatican officials into a reactive mode. The men apparently realize that the days of women cooperating in their own oppression are numbered and the time of women acting as full moral agents is at hand.

Thanks to Pope Francis, men's constrictions on women's role in the Church may be coming to an end. As Sister Beatrix Mayrhofer, president of the Association of Austrian Women Religious, said at a book presentation on May 20, 2016,

> *"Women religious have ceased to be just kindergarten teachers, cooks, cleaning ladies or women sextons. We must break out of these clerical mid-level positions and say, "Dear men colleagues, your image of women religious is a relic of the old seminary times. Today you must clean the sacristy your-*

selves. The traditional image is still deeply entrenched within the Church itself. As long as women religious continue to play their old roles, to a certain extent they are to blame."

Catholics who are concerned about the number of young women no longer passing through the doors of the Church, as well as the future of the Church, are taking action. Twenty-seven Catholic organizations have drawn up a Declaration for our daughters that will be delivered to the United States bishops at their June, 2016 assembly, asking them to build a Church for its daughters in the future.

On January 6, 2016 Pope Francis issued a Decree stating women should be included in the foot-washing rites held on Holy Thursday.

On May 13, 2016 Pope Francis announced that he would create a commission to study ordaining women as Deacons. Loretta Duquette, the subject of Chapter 20, served as a Lay Ecclesial Minister. She told me that she is now taking a course on Spirituality and is ready to accept elevation to deacon, if and when Pope Francis makes the proclamation.

An editorial in the May 8-21, 2015 issue of the *National Catholic Reporter*, commenting on the conflict between the Vatican and the U.S women religious, stated, "The Congregation for the Doctrine of the Faith's 'assessment' of LCWR was a disaster, an unnecessary sign of mistrust....If there is reason to cheer, it is that the women managed to impress on the Vatican that they had no intention of engaging the issue exclusively on the arcane protocol of an all-male culture, in which only its members are clued in to the means of survival. So the women hold out for the conversation of equals...We could easily make the case that these sisters have a true reading on the beating heart of the church...But the sisters can do more in governance than to advise a man. That is absurd. The inclusion of women into leadership ranks of the Church won't be easy—reform and renewal never are—but it is essential."

Pope Francis, continue to listen to your Commission on the feasibility of ordaining women as deacons of the Church. It is essential to the renewal and growth of our spiritual family, the Catholic Church.

END NOTES

INTRODUCTION

[1] Janice Sevre-Duszynska, NCR: 12/5/14

[2] Judy Vaughan's biography of Marge Tuite, OP, (1922-1986) Women and Leadership Archives, Loyola University Chicago, Collection 1917-1988

CHAPTER ONE

[1] "A landmark, ground-breaking classic—these adjectives barely do justice to the pioneering vision and lasting impact of The Feminine Mystique – Gail Collins O Magazine introduction to the 50th anniversary of the book publication on February, 2013

[2] Arianna Huffington in O Magazine February 2013 on The Feminine Mystique – "forever changed the conversation as well as the way women view themselves...it is a great moment to celebrate this milestone work which fundamentally altered the course of women's lives."

CHAPTER TWO

[1] Helen Ring Robinson's letter to Mrs. N.M. Jarger, editor of the *Pictorial Review, May, 1919, P21*

[2] Carol Gilligan, Psychologist: *In a Different Voice: Psychological Theory and Women's Development.* Harvard University Press, 1982

CHAPTER THREE

[1] Erika Bachiochi, *Women, Sex and the Church:* Pauline Books and Media, Boston, MA. 2010

[2] Bishop Kevin C. Rhoades, Chairman of the United States Bishops' Committee on the Laity, Marriage, Family Life and Youth. *A Good Marriage Goes a Long Way;* October 3,2011

[3] Angela Franks, Ph.D., *The Gift of Female Fertility: Church Teaching on Contraception*: Pauline Books 2010

[4] Helen M. Alvere J.D., N*National Catholic Reporter*: September 11, 2012

CHAPTER FIVE

[1] Katinka Hesselink: A student of several religions, Published *Essays on Karma*, 2014.

[2] Ibid.

[3] Wikipedia: LCWR: Founded in 1956 to assist its members in carrying out its mission.

[4] Sister Joan Kelleher Doyle, BVM, LCWR President, LCWR conference 1978. (Wikipedia)

[5] Arthur Jones, NCR staff, *National Catholic Reporter: September 8, 2000*

CHAPTER SIX

[1] Vita Consecrata 1996 #46)

[2] Jason Berry: NCR, June 28, 2013

[3] Sister Pat Farrell address, "Navigating The Shifts": Joshua McElweek, NCR journalist April 26, 2012

[4] Bishops Accountability.org: December 2, 2013.

CHAPTER SEVEN

[1] *Italian Daily*: Corriere della serra interview of Cardinal Carlo Maria Martini, S.J., hours before his death on August 31, 2012

[2] Nuns on the Bus: "An Evening with Sister and Spirits" Rochester, NY, October 21, 2016

[3] Jason Berry, Journalist, National Catholic Reporter, January 18-31, 2013

[4] Ibid

[5] Ibid

CHAPTER EIGHT

1 USCCB – Pope John Paul II's document: Ordinatio Sacerdotalis, May 22, 1994

2 New documents illustrating early Christianity, G.H.R., Horsley publisher, 1976

CHAPTER NINE

1 Catholic Youth Organization to become active in her adult years to shaping theology

2 Ibid

3 John L. Allen, Jr. *National Catholic Reporter*, Journalist, 2008

4 Elizabeth Schussler Fiorenza, *In Memory of Her: A Feministic Theological Reconstruction of Christian Origins*, Crossroads, 1994

CHAPTER TEN

1 Sarah Durant, author, broadcaster and writer for the Royal Academy Magazine November 12, 2015

2 Ibid

3 The Vatican Synod on the Family

4 Ibid

5 Reverend Roy Donovan, a signer of the letter sent by twelve Irish priests condemning the "oppression of women within the Catholic Church"

CHAPTER ELEVEN

1 Whispering Hope: *The Heartbreaking True Story Of The Magdalene Women* by Costello, Nancy; Legg, Kathleen; Croughan, Diane; Slattery, Marie; Gambold, Mari, Kan. Orion, 2016

2 Ibid

3 Ibid

4 Stephen O'Leary: *The Irish Times* August 19, 2013

[5] Prime minister Enda Kenny and the Irish Government agree to compensating the Magdalene Laundry survivors.

CHAPTER TWELVE

[1] Saint Benedict wrote his Rule in the ordinary Latin of the day, between 530 A.D. and 560 A.D.

[2] Holy Wisdom (Ecumenical) Monastery in Madison, Wisconsin, which was environmentally friendly opened in the fall of 2009

[3] Louf, A.A: *Teach Us To Pray:Learning A Little About Prayer,* December 1974

[4] Father Richard Rohr's meditations *Daily Reflections of Your Soul.*

CHAPTER THIRTEEN

[1] Michael Kelly, editor of T*he Irish Catholic,* interviewing Mary McAleese, former President of Ireland, 2015

[2] Heidi Schlumpf, *National Catholic Reporter,* December 3, 2015

[3] NCR, the National Press Club, September 17, 2015

[4] *The Wall Street Journal,* Melanie Grayce West interview of Sister Donna Markham, October 2, 2015

[5] CNS News: Terence P Jeffrey, June 10, 2015

[6] *Global Sisters Report,* NCR, February 7, 2015

[7] Thomas C. Fox, *Global Sisters Report,* National Catholic Reporter, Sister Carmen Sammut addressing the Union of International Superior Generals February 6, 2015

CHAPTER FOURTEEN

[1] Elizabeth A. Dryer, Associate Professor in the Department of Religious Studies at Fairfield University, Connecticut – *American Magazine* "In the Tradition of Sister Madeleva" June 17, 2000

CHAPTER FIFTEEN

[1] Tom Roberts, *National Catholic Reporter,* December April 17, 2015

[2] Ibid

[3] Tom Roberts, *National Catholic Reporter*, December 1, 2015

[4] Ibid

[5] Ibid

[6] Ibid

[7] Massimo Faggioli, *The Huffington Post*, May 9, 2016

CHAPTER SIXTEEN

[1] Muslim women fight to redefine Islam in terms of equality.
TIME magazine, March 23, 2015

[2] Reverend Dr. Susan Brooks, Thistlewaite "Stop Using Religion to Justify Violence Against Women" *The Huffington Post*, September 7, 2015

[3] The Huffington Post, March 8, 2016

[4] Dr. Alison Boden, Dean of Religious Life, Princeton University, T*he Arab Spring and Human Rights*, January 14, 2013

CHAPTER SEVENTEEN

[1] Monica Migliorino Miller, *The Authority of Women in the Catholic Church* (Steubenville, Ohio: Emmaus Road, 2015).

[2] Edith Stein, *Essays On Woman* (The Collected Works of Edith Stein Book 2) (Washington, D.C.: ICS Publications, 1987) 230

[3] Elizabeth A. Johnson, *She Who Is: The Mystery of God in Feminist Theological Discourse* (The Crossroad Publishing Company, 1993) 26

[4] Miller

[5] Austin Flannery, O.P., Vatican Council II, Vol. 2: More Post Conciliar Documents (Collegeville, MN: Costello Publishing Company, 1982) 340

CHAPTER EIGHTEEN

[1] NCR Staff, "Review *National Catholic Reporter* Coverage of Women Deacons," *National Catholic Reporter*, May 12, 2016.

[2] Ibid

[3] Ibid

4 Dr. Thomas Groome, Director of the Church in the 21st Century.

5 Jonathan Pitts, At St Pius X Catholic Church, top official is a woman, *The Baltimore Sun*, February 26, 2016.

6 Ibid

7 Ibid

CHAPTER NINETEEN
1 Historian Margaret Ward: *In Their Own Voice: Women and Irish Nationalism*, publisher Attic Press: December 31, 2001

2 Johanna Sheehy Skeffington: *A Life* (Cork University Press, 1997)

3 Padraig Pearse: "Proclamation at the General Post Office (G.P.O.) on Monday, April 24, 1916 The Irish Independent Newspaper

4 Dr. Monica Migliorino Miller, *The Authority of Women in the Catholic Church*, Steubenville, Ohio: Emmaus Road Publishing, 2015

5 *Irish Central Company* November 3, 2015 "12 Priests Call For An End Of 'Oppression' Of Women By Catholic Church"

CHAPTER TWENTY
1 USCCB subcommittee on lay ministry Co-Workers in the Vineyard of the Lord: A Resource for Guiding the Development of Lay Ecclesial Ministry, Washington, D.C, USCCB Publishing
2 Ibid

3 Loretta's schedule as a Lay Ecclesial Minister

CHAPTER TWENTY-ONE
1 Global Sister Report, *National Catholic Reporter*, "Sisters of CMSWR Explore Prophetic Character of Religious Life at St. Louis Symposium"

(November 13, 2015 – Dawn Araujo-Hawkins reporting)

[2] Ibid

[3] Ibid

CHAPTER TWENTY-TWO

[1] The words "holon" and "holarchy" were created by Arthur Koestler in Ghost and the Machine (1967). A holon is natural organism, composed of semi-autonomous sub-wholes, linked together to form a hierarchy. To create a holarchy is to form a whole.

[2] Ilia Delio, Making *All Things New, Catholicity, Cosmology, Consciousness* (2015). Orbis.

[3] Leonard Swiller: T*he Dialogue of Decalogue: Ground Rules for Interreligious Dialogue Journal of Ecumenical Studies*: Winter 1983.

[4] Ibid... Ilia Delio. Page 136

[5] (Wikepedia, March 1, 2016)

[6] *National Catholic Reporter* January 29, 2016.

[7] *National Catholic Reporter* December 2, 2013.

[8] Ibid.,

[9] (Dunne, November 8, 2013) *National Catholic Reporter* (NCR)

[10] Ibid.

[11] NCR, March 27, 2015

[12] Austen Ivereigh, *The Great Reformer: Francis and the Making of a Radical Pope* (2014).

[13] Ibid.

EPILOGUE

[1] John J. Fialka, Sisters: *Catholic Nuns and the Making of America* (McLean, VA: St. Martin's Press, 2003)

[2] Michael O'Loughlin, "Women Lead In The Church, Even As Catholics Debate Their Role," *CRUX Magazine*, January 15, 2015

[3] Jessica Zigmond, More Long-time Care Upheaval: Modern Healthcare magazine, August 27, 2007.

[4] Dr. Carolyn Woo: "Working for a Better World," (Our Sunday Visitor, Publishing Division, 2015)

[5] Anne E. Patrick, *Conscience and Calling: Ethical Reflections on Catholic Women's Church Vocations* (New York: Bloomsbury Publishing, 2013)

[6] Jamie Manson, Sister Anne E. Patrick Receives John Courtney Murray Award, *National Catholic Reporter*, June 9, 2013

[7] Mary E. Hunt: Author Connects The Dots Of Sisters' Evolution: *National Catholic Reporter*, July 4-17, 2014

[8] Christa Pongratz-Lippitt, "Shortcomings Of Women's Role In The Church Coming To An End," *National Catholic Reporter*, May 25, 2016

[9] *National Catholic Reporter* Editorial Staff, "Hierarchy's Flaws Persist Despite Collegial End To LCWR Investigation," *National Catholic Reporter*, May 8-21, 2015

Finbarr M. Corr, Ed. D. was born in County Cavan, Ireland, one of nine Children to John Francis Corr and Nell (Doyle) Corr. He attended the local public school, which had two classrooms, two teachers and was managed by the local parish priest. He attended St. Patrick's College Cavan for five years, followed by six years at the seminary, St Patrick's College Carlow. He was ordained a priest in June 1960 and emigrated to New Jersey as a 'missionary' priest in August 1960.

He served as an associate pastor in an inner city parish in the Paterson Diocese for six years, followed by three years in a suburban parish in Morristown NJ. He received a master's degree in Pastoral Counseling and an Ed.D. in Family Life Education. In 1969 he was appointed the first fulltime director of the Family Life Bureau for the Diocese of Paterson, with the responsibility of creating family life programs throughout the three county diocese. He was appointed pastor of St. Vincent Martyr Parish, Madison, NJ in 1979, where he created a pastoral team, to administer the parish of 1800 families.

He resigned the priesthood in June 1988 and married Laurie Hutton. He initiated his own Marriage and Family counseling program called "Partners in Change," providing counseling for couples and families from parishes and student assistance programs for Catholic high schools. He is the author of eight books and lives on Cape Cod with his wife Laurie and both spend winters in Fort Meyers FL.

www.finbarrcorr.com

His books are available on www.amazon.com.

A Kid from Legaginney is available from Amazon

When Dr. Finbarr Corr published the first edition of his autobiography in 2003, *A Kid from Legaginney*, he was surprised at its success, as he never thought of himself as a proficient student in English literature. Author Frank McCourt, who inspired Dr. Corr to write and disagrees with his self-assessment, endorsed the second edition saying

> "*A Kid from Legaginney is warm and leavened with gentle breezes of kindness, humor, and compassion. Here is a memoir of a man, doing God's work, a man with a great heart and writing style, that draws you in, as if you were sitting by his fireside listening. Listening and being moved.*"

BROKEN PROMISES:
Whatever happened to Vatican Council II?

"The Catholic hierarchy's failure to follow through on the mandate of Vatican Council II to open up the Church is the most critical missed opportunity for the Church in contemporary times. The simultaneous cover-up by the hierarchy of pedophile priests is most damaging and threatens the very survival of our Church. Our hopes are focused now on the People of God calling for Vatican Council III to save Catholicism."

Finbarr M Corr Ed. D.

Broken Promises ... Whatever happened to Vatican Council II?

is available from Amazon

Finbarr M. Corr Ed. D. was motivated to write Broken
Promises...Whatever happened to Vatican Council II?
by his early experiences as a priest in the Diocese of
Paterson, New Jersey and the ministry and leadership of Saint Pope John
XXIII, during Vatican Council II (1962-65).

Dr. Corr offered his first mass in Latin in Ireland on June 12, 1960.
Less than two years later, the newly elected Pope John XXIII declared to
his fellow bishops, it is time to "open the windows of the Church and let
in some fresh air"...He initiated Vatican Council II, which changed the
definition of the Church to the "People of God," thus sharing the
authority, traditionally held by the hierarchy, with lay Catholics. Dr.
Corr now enjoyed celebrating mass in the vernacular and preaching
that "The Church is not its buildings but is, in reality, only living stones,
its people, who are "called out of darkness into His wonderful light".
(Peter 2:8-9)

Unfortunately, Pope John didn't live long enough to orchestrate the
renewal of his beloved Catholic Church. He died in 1963, and his successors didn't follow through on the promises of Vatican Council II.

Dr. Corr examines "the ongoing conflict between the top-down,
authoritative model of the Church administration and the bottom-up,
democratic model that Pope John XXIII envisioned for the renewed
People of God, a priesthood in whereby the laity would openly share
with the ministerial priesthood in both Church administration and dis-
cernment about the Church's role in the context of modern society."

43038197R00110

Made in the USA
Middletown, DE
28 April 2017